Practicing Principals

Case Studies, In-Baskets, and Policy Analysis

Perry R. Rettig

ScarecrowEducation
Lanham, Maryland • Toronto • Oxford
2004

Published in the United States of America
by ScarecrowEducation
An imprint of The Rowman & Littlefield Publishing Group, Inc.
4501 Forbes Boulevard, Suite 200, Lanham, Maryland 20706
www.scaroweducation.com

PO Box 317
Oxford
OX2 9RU, UK

British Library Cataloguing in Publication Information Available

Library of Congress Cataloging-in-Publication Data

Rettig, Perry Richard.
    Practicing principals : case studies, in-baskets, and policy analysis
/ Perry R. Rettig.
        p. cm.
    Includes bibliographical references and index.
    ISBN 1-57886-113-6 (pbk. : alk. paper)
    1. School principals—United States—Handbooks, manuals, etc. 2.
School principals—Training of—United States. I. Title.
LB2831.92 .R48 2004
371.2'012—dc22

                                    2003025267

This book is dedicated to my students and colleagues. Their dedication to educational leadership is both inspiring and encouraging for our future.

Contents

Introduction   vii

Case Studies and In-Basket Activities   1

Case Categories   79

List of Cases   81

References   85

Index   87

About the Author   89

Introduction

Current administrators, board of education members, and professional associations alike are calling for future principals to have at least a modicum of real-life experience when they enter their first administrative assignments. We hear that preservice principals may know administrative theory, but they have no practical experience to serve as a context for this knowledge. In the words of Robert Owens, "We are continually confronted by evidence that academic assumptions often contrast remarkably with the experiences of individuals engaged in the work of school administration" (2004, p. 157). This book allows you the opportunity to experience real-life issues of a typical school principal. But more important, it allows you the chance to practice under the protection of time and under the guidance of a mentor.

The case study approach has come to be known as an excellent vehicle for preservice administrators to practice their future craft in a safe environment—one that allows for introspection and second chances. Whereas most books of case studies and in-basket activities are arranged around themes and topics, this book is arranged around realistic and pragmatic experiences of practitioners. Themes and topics are brought forth in this context.

Practicing Principals contains a series of case studies, in-baskets, and policy analysis activities for you to discuss with your peer group. You have the opportunity to sit back and examine these situations in a variety of ways. For example, under the guidance of your instructor, you may analyze each situation through the lenses of different leadership, organizational, and motivation theories. You will engage in the praxis as described by Paulo Freire (2002). In other words, you will be continually asked to reflect on your beliefs and values of school leadership and then put those philosophical presuppositions into practice by completing the in-baskets and case studies. With this approach you will be able to connect theory and practice and to apply them to your context, not someone else's. It is recommended that you do the activities in the book using the policies, procedures, and protocol in your own district. Likewise, it would be extremely beneficial for you to discuss each case activity with your own principal, in order to get a current practitioner's view.

Case studies require you to engage in a sophisticated mix of reflection and action of complex issues that inservice building administrators deal with on a daily basis. Such case studies require active learners, not passive note-takers. Great interaction occurs with peers. But, please avoid simple sharing of opinions. It is important to see how congruent your responses are to your espoused beliefs and values. To avoid purely relativistic answers based solely on your hunches, it is important for you to prepare for these cases by articulating your leadership philosophies. To create this baseline thinking, you are asked to respond to the tasks put forth at the end of this introduction. You may find it a valuable experience to revisit these tasks after you have completed all the work in this book.

Practicing Principals is written from the perspective of a new middle school principal, Ms. Leslie O'Connor. This approach will put the various activities into a relatively realistic context. You can then examine how Leslie handled the situations and how you might handle them differently. If you are an elementary school or high school educator, you may wish to modify some of the situations to better frame their context. Finally, while it is intended that you will move through this book in a sequential order, it would be justifiable to jump around to meet your needs.

In preparation for this book, I read a book edited by N. Katherine Hayles titled, *Chaos and Order: Complex Dynamics in Literature and Science.* In a chapter titled "The Chaos of Metafiction," Peter Stoicheff beautifully captures the essence of the reason I have chosen to write *Practicing Principals* in this narrative fashion:

To understand a metafictional text, one must reject seeing it as a vertical organization of a text's components into a closed order that is interpreted as meaning. Rather, one places this view with the recognition of lateral patterns in which disorder becomes order, mystery becomes illumination and then fragments into a new disorder. This pattern generates the reader's continual interpretation of the metafictional text and also the text's self-generation, for the pattern is a manifestation of the text's reading of itself.

So, while there is a linear aspect to this book—its chronological movement—it is more natural and authentic in its approach to the characters' (and I might add—to your) experiences. In other words, the content is not smooth and linear. Issues and tasks emerge as they do in real life. They may appear disjointed and chaotic, but overall patterns begin to appear. At the same time, I have tried to incorporate the theoretical constructs taught in educational leadership and administration courses. I have tried to leave a taste of realism for you and allow you to explore these concepts and ideas on your own and with the guidance of your professors.

When approaching these cases, you might find it beneficial to think about the following questions: What is the relevant information? What other information is still needed or desired? Whom should I contact for this information or for advice? Who is necessary to involve in the decision? What will be my approach to my decision-making? What are my options? What is my choice and why? An index of categories of case studies, mini-cases, in-baskets, and policies is included for your convenience and as a quick reference.

BACKGROUND

Ms. Leslie O'Connor had been a science teacher for the past five years in nearby Brementon while she finished her master's degree and administrator certification. Now she has been hired as the new principal at Lancaster Middle School in the Britton Area School District one week prior to the beginning of this school year. She is replacing former principal Ben Richards. Leslie has no prior relationships with any of the employees in the school district. Ron Cartwright is the assistant principal, and Georgine Simons is her secretary.

Note

You should consider the community of Britton, the school district, and Lancaster Middle School to be a mirror image of your own setting. In other words, if you are from a large urban community, you should consider that to be the context of Leslie's principalship. Or, if you are from a rural or suburban community, you should consider that to be the context for the activities in this book.

QUESTIONS TO PREPARE YOU FOR THE CASE STUDIES

To best prepare for the case studies, in-baskets, and policy analysis activities, it will be beneficial to spend some time reflecting on your educational leadership philosophies in several areas. So, please take some time to write responses to these questions. Then, as you move forward into the book, keep in mind what you have now espoused. In this way, it is hoped, your actions will be congruent with your values and beliefs.

1. Douglas McGregor developed a model to help us characterize what we believe about human motivation. As a supervisor of employees, it is very important that you fully recognize your underlying assumptions about people. Once you are cognizant of your beliefs, you can make appropriate and congruent decisions. McGregor explained that if you believe people are inherently lazy, self-centered, weak, and selfishly competitive, and need to be motivated externally, you are a proponent of Theory X.

   On the other hand, Theory Y stipulates that people are inherently good, self-motivated, goal-oriented, cooperative, and hardworking. If people show characteristics of the negative behaviors mentioned in Theory X, it is because their work experiences have created such conditions.

   With that said, what do you believe about human nature? Are you more aligned with Theory X or Y? Then, what does this mean to your leadership in terms of staff motivation, teacher supervision and evaluation, and decision-making?

2. The requirements of today's principals require a fine mixture of leadership and management characteristics. Dr. John Kotter of the Harvard University Business School clearly elucidated the trait differences between leaders and managers (1999).

Managers	Leaders
status quo	change
planning and budgeting	setting direction
organizing and staffing	aligning people
controlling/problem-solving	motivating and inspiring
deductive	inductive

Do you agree with Kotter's concept of the differences between managers and leaders? What changes/additions would you make? Most important, which responsibilities of the building administrator would you consider to be more management-oriented and which more leadership-oriented? For example, as you will supervise and evaluate staff, put together and administer your budget, chair committees, make decisions, communicate with various groups, and so on, will you serve more in the role of leader or manager? Take the time to write down your thoughts on these matters. As you progress to the case study activities, keep these thoughts in mind.

3. Carl Glickman, Stephen Gordon, and Jovita M. Ross-Gordon (1998) have created a model for how principals can differentiate their supervision of instruction approaches depending on different teachers' needs. This same model could be applied, in my estimation, to all interactions principals have with their employees.

   With this model, some teachers need a great deal of supervision from their principal. The approach the supervisor would use is called *directive control*. Here, the supervisor takes on the responsibility of explaining expectations to the employee. When the employee is able to take on slightly more responsibility, the administrator would use the approach called *directive informational*. Here, it is expected that the supervisor provide appropriate information to assist the employee to begin to take on more ownership.

The third category along this continuum is called *collaborative*. This approach is clearly distinct in that the supervisor and employee work together in a sharing of responsibility; it's a partnership. The ultimate approach on this continuum of supervisory behavior is the approach called *nondirective*. Here, employees have the experience and expertise to be self-directing. They take on the responsibility and indicate the assistance, as appropriate, they need from the administrator. This is the master teacher and true professional.

For your reflection here, consider how you would use this conceptual model. Where would you place different people in your current situation along this continuum? What type of interactions/duties of the principal would require such a differentiated approach to working with employees?

4. Thomas Sergiovanni and Robert Starratt (2002) talk of the need for school leaders to take the time to develop a supervisor's platform. I would like to refocus this reflective tool to help you think about your administrative interaction with employees, rather than just supervision of instruction. This new platform is an analysis of your philosophy of supervisory behavior coupled with a description of how you would put it into practice.

For this activity, write your own supervisor's platform. There are two parts to this platform. Begin by writing your philosophy of the principal's role in supervisory interactions with employees. In other words, what is the role of the leader when working with different people? Then, write about the manner in which you would lead different people in your building. For example, how will you interact with various people who are at different places on Glickman, Gordon, and Ross-Gordon's continuum? Do specific situations require different responses? If so, how?

5. Now that you have taken the time to reflect on your educational leadership philosophies, it is important to think about your leadership style or approach. I'm referring to the way in which you will carry out your espoused leadership beliefs every day.

Dan Goleman (2000) explicated six leadership styles: *coercive, authoritative, affiliative, democratic, pacesetting,* and *coaching.* Coercive leaders demand immediate compliance, while authoritative leaders mobilize people. Affiliative leaders create harmony and build emotional bonds, while democratic leaders forge consensus through participation. Finally, pacesetting leaders set high standards for performance, while coaching leaders develop people for the future.

Perhaps you have studied or prefer other leadership style descriptions. For example, you may consider that requirements for leadership styles depend on the complexities of differing situations. If so, then the Situational Leadership Model from Hersey and Blanchard (1988) is the approach you espouse. Here, each unique situation is a blend between a needed emphasis on task and on relationships. The first style is *autocratic directive,* where the emphasis is high on task and low on relationships. The *democratic collaborative* style emphasizes both high task and high relationship. Encouraging *nondirective* leaders focus low on task and high on relationships. Finally, *laissez-faire* leaders have a low emphasis on both task and relationship. The idea with situational leadership is that the leader identifies both the ability and willingness of employees to accomplish a task at hand. The principal then uses a style most appropriate for the given situation.

A slightly different way of looking at how administrators adjust their leadership styles to the situations they and their employees face is called the Path–Goal Contingency Model. Robert House and Terrence Mitchell (1974) described four leadership styles: The leader in the *directive* style clearly tells the workers what is expected of them. In the *supportive* style, the supervisor is friendly and supportive in helping the workers complete the necessary tasks. In the third approach, the *participative* style, the administrator asks the workers for active engagement in decision-making while still maintaining ultimate authority. The final approach is the *achievement*-oriented style. Here, the leader challenges and supports the workers in their pursuit of the goals at hand. Again, the situation calls for different leadership styles.

While there may be numerous ways to look at leadership styles or approaches, it is important for you to consider which type you would use on a daily basis. Please spend some time, now, in reflecting upon what style you will use. Will it be one consistent approach or will it vary depending on the situations you will face? You may want to consider such issues as committee leadership, working with difficult staff members, creating vision, and leading reform.

6. Often and routinely you will be challenged as you carry out your leadership style. Managing conflict will be critical to your work. When your leadership is challenged, you may choose to *avoid* the problem, you may choose to make a *compromise*, or you may choose to *compete* in a win-lose approach. Likewise, you may choose to make *accommodations* or to be *collaborative*.

Please spend some time describing these five different ways of dealing with conflict. Then, explain where each one may be appropriate to use, as well as problems associated with that approach. Finally, spend a few moments considering the one approach that you typically use. For example, do you normally avoid conflict or find yourself using a competitive approach? Knowing the answer, what will this mean to your approach in dealing with conflict in the future?

7. One final task before you move on to the case activities. Building administrators make literally hundreds of decisions daily. Often, students in educational administration courses are taught a rational decision-making approach. In such a model, principals first define the problem, then analyze it. Next, they develop alternative solutions, and then choose the best solution. They conclude this process by taking the appropriate action based on their rational analysis.

More contemporary thinking for decision-making observes that leaders don't make routine decisions in a rational and analytical way. Rather, administrators are confronted with extraordinarily complex situations with unclear goals and variables. Even more, they often are unaware of all the facts and are faced with emotional people who have hidden agendas. Quite frankly, while we would like to believe that decision-making is logical and rational, it is most often not. In real life, people's decision-making is more often unclear, untidy, and nonrational. With this understanding of decision-making, the leader must consider such issues as who should be involved in the decision, what information is needed, what is not known, and what are the ramifications of the decision?

Your final task is for you to consider the most appropriate way to make decisions. Please think about whether it is best to have one approach or whether different situations call for different approaches. What things do you need to consider? Finally, as you move forward in tackling the case activities, use your espoused approach to decision-making as a guide.

The real voyage in discovery
Consists not in seeking new landscapes,
But in having new eyes.

— Marcel Proust

1. MINI-CASE

Dr. Tony Mousseli is the superintendent of the Britton Area School District. Immediately upon hiring Leslie O'Connor as the new principal at Lancaster Middle School, he wrote a memorandum to the school staff. Box 1 shows that memo announcing the appointment of Leslie O'Connor as principal.

Your Task

Critique this memo from Dr. Mousseli. Would you write a memo or handle it in a different manner? Either write your own memo or show

---

Box 1 Memo to the Staff

To: Lancaster School Staff
From: Dr. Tony Mousseli
Re: New Principal
Date: August 24

The Britton School District administrative team is pleased to announce that we have appointed Ms. Leslie O'Connor as the new principal at Lancaster School effective immediately.

Ms. O'Connor has taught seventh-grade science for our rival, the Brementon Lions, for the past five years. She earned her master's degree in educational leadership and principal certification from Central State University. Please join us in welcoming Leslie to this new administrative position.

---

what you would do differently. You may wish to consider which leadership theory or model Dr. Mousseli follows. Likewise, you might want to consider how your approach to this announcement is congruent with the leadership theory/model you espouse.

2. MINI-CASE

On Saturday morning, Leslie visited her new school to become acquainted with her surroundings. New teachers arrive for districtwide inservice meetings on Wednesday morning and are to go to their schools in the afternoon to meet with their principals and mentors. On Thursday morning, all teachers report back for the annual State of the District address by Dr. Mousseli in the high school auditorium. In the afternoon, all professional staff members are to attend faculty meetings at their own schools. Friday is reserved for teachers to have time to work in their classrooms. Paraprofessionals return to work on Friday, while the secretarial staff has been working since last Monday. The custodial staff has been working throughout the summer.

Box 2   Letter from the New Principal

Welcome back!

Please allow me to introduce myself. I am Leslie O'Connor, and I am your new principal. I have been a teacher in Brementon before coming to Lancaster and have received my administrative master's degree and certification at Central State University.

Lancaster has earned a wonderful reputation, and it is my plan to continue its tradition of excellence. To that end, I would like to invite all faculty to the school cafeteria next Saturday at 8 a.m. where I will serve you a nutritious, and I hope delicious, breakfast. After breakfast we can talk about goals for the year and new policies that will affect us all.

I look forward to meeting each of you and to a great school year.

Sincerely,
Leslie O'Connor
Principal

Leslie looked on her desk and saw the memo from Tony Mousseli announcing her hiring. She felt a little miffed since she wanted to make the announcement. But she decided to go ahead and write a letter to her staff herself, anyway. The letter is shown in box 2.

Your Task

Draft a letter that you will send to your staff announcing yourself as the new principal. What things do you need to include in this letter? Will you consider including items about meetings, schedules, and so on?

3. MINI-CASE

Sitting behind her desk, Leslie turned on her PDA and looked at the notes she had written as a "to do" list for herself. She saw a seemingly chaotic list staring at her:

- Meet with assistant principal—Ron Cartwright.
- Assign mentor to new LD teacher—Elton Burrows.
- Review district policy manual.
- Review district supervision/evaluation procedures.
- Write parent newsletter.
- Call PTO president.
- Ask secretary whether all supplies have arrived.
- Ask custodian whether everything is set for first day of school.
- Set up appointment with district curriculum director to learn about all the curricular areas.
- Set up appointment with my mentor.

Your Task

First, edit this list by adding and deleting items that you will address upon getting your first building administrator assignment. Second, list the items that you would like to talk to your assistant principal about. Then, describe what characteristics you would look for in a mentor for a new teacher. Since there is no other LD teacher in your building, would you use an LD teacher from another building as a mentor or stay with a non-LD teacher from within your own building?

Obviously, your district policy manual will be too cumbersome to review each and every policy. Explain which policies you will want to review first. Next, list the items you wish to consider for your first parent newsletter.

Now, detail any questions and directives you will discuss with your custodian, your secretary, the PTO president, and the district curriculum coordinator.

Finally, meet with the current principal and discuss the issues set forth here. For example, how does she or he choose mentors? What policies does she or he think are the most imperative to become familiar with? What things would she or he consider crucial for your first parent newsletter? What items would she or he be certain to discuss with the secretary, custodian, PTO president, and district curriculum coordinator?

4. IN-BASKET

After Leslie checked off the items on her list, she turned to a variety of notes, letters, and memoranda sitting on her desk (see box 3).

Box 3   In-Basket

1. Phone call
Anonymous caller complaining about he doesn't want the same problems from last year's football team to happen again. This is in reference to after school problems where several football players harassed and swore at members of the other sports teams—no real supervision.

2. Letter
July 28
Dear Principal:
As you may know, our family belongs to the Fundamentalist Church of Our Savior. We are always deeply concerned about the secular nature of our public schools and of the nihilistic approach to teaching in your school system. If we could afford

---

to send our children to a God-fearing parochial school, we would.

Your eighth-grade teacher recently sent out a letter to all parents of his incoming students telling about the new textbook for his social studies class. It is my understanding that he plans to skip parts of the textbook that has been adopted by the board of education and use this new book as the primary text. We are appalled at the revisionist approach to history found in this new book—our church has warned us about it. We want you to have that book removed from the classroom as it was not adopted by the board of education. We also want the teacher to thoroughly complete the first textbook, which was adopted by the board of education.

Yours in faith,
Mr. and Mrs. Tony Premfield
cc: Superintendent
Board of Education members

3. Phone call
Return phone call of Mr. Oren Maplethord, president of school board. 555-5666

4. E-mail (Friday 10:48 pm)
Dear Ms. O'Connor,
I represent a group of concerned citizens in the county. We are concerned about the use of an Indian Warrior as your school's mascot. We find such depictions of Native Americans insensitive and inappropriate. We will be happy to work with you this year in choosing a more appropriate and suitable mascot. I look forward to hearing from you.

Most sincerely,
Madeline Zckeriak

5. Phone call
Mr. Harwell from the newspaper called. He wants to talk to you about the Indian Chief logo at your school. 555-4321

6. Phone call
George Henry, Esq. called. He represents the State Taxpayers' Alliance. They want to look at your school budget according to the Public Records Act. He will be here sometime Monday morning.

(*continued*)

Box 3 In-Basket (*continued*)

7. E-mail
To: All Principals
From: Tony Mousseli, Superintendent BASD
Re: Emergency Meeting
Date: Friday
Indeed, the worst-case scenario looks to be coming true. We received word today from the state that school districts must reduce their budgets by 5 percent. As the school year is upon us, contracts have already been signed and most purchases have been made. This will be extremely difficult. Therefore, we will hold an emergency meeting at 7:30 a.m. Monday for the entire administrative staff team. Please bring your ideas for reducing your building/location budget by 5 percent. Nothing will be sacred.

8. E-mail (August 21)
Welcome, Ms. O'Connor,
I don't know if you are aware, but we had worked out an arrangement with former Lancaster Principal Ben Richards to have your playground equipment upgraded this summer! The good news is that the materials are due any day now. The bad news is that we won't be able to get to the job of installation until the second week of school. It is my estimation that the job will take us four or five days, during which time you will need to shut down the playground. I want to let you know about this early enough so that you can plan accordingly. If you should have any questions, please feel free to contact me.

Sincerely,
Murphy McKenzey
Coordinator of Buildings and Grounds

9. Phone Message
Mrs. Beatrice Snow called. 555-4728. She is upset that kids will again be using her yard as a shortcut on the way home from school. What are you going to do about it?

10. Message from Your Secretary
Some teachers have complained in the past, and I agree with them, that some of the kids get dropped off at school too early in

the morning. They aren't supposed to be here before 7:45, but some kids are here as early as 7:15. Do you want to write something for the parent newsletter?

11. Handwritten Note from a Teacher

I don't know if you are aware of this, but the teacher across from me, Joy Hammer, has always arrived to school routinely late. By contract we are supposed to be here by 7:30, but she doesn't usually get here until 8:00. This is a direct affront to the principal's authority. I thought you would like to know so this problem doesn't happen this year. By the way, please don't share this with her. I have to work closely with her and don't want to be caught in the middle.

Vickie Albertson

12. Letter

Dear Principal:

I hope this letter reaches you in the best of health and ready for your new school year.

Please allow me to introduce myself, I am Beatrice Williams, president of the Ladies Auxiliary. At each month's meeting, we invite a guest to speak to our members over the lunch hour. We would love to hear your fresh perspectives on the future of education. Our meeting will be held two weeks from Thursday at the Shangri-La Gardens. Would you be so kind as to accept our invitation?

Most sincerely,
Beatrice Williams

13. Letter

Dear Principal O'Connor,

I hope you are enjoying your school year. I have a business proposition for you. If you sell only our soda products in your school, we will provide a free scoreboard for your gym.

Sincerely,
Bob Whipple
Fruity-Juice Soda

Your Task

Handle each "in-basket" item as you really would in your new position. For example, if you would respond to a person with a letter, a memo, or an e-mail, actually write that letter, memo, or e-mail. If you were to make a phone call, write the questions or points you would like to make. If you were to add some of these items to your first faculty meeting agenda, actually put together that agenda and describe the points you plan to make about those agenda items. While you're at it, go ahead and fully put together your first faculty meeting agenda. Finally, prioritize each in-basket item as a 1, 2, or 3. Items that you number with a 1 are Urgent and you will complete them before you go home tonight. Items that are numbered 2 (Important) are things that you will take care of on Monday. Items with a 3 priority (Can Wait) can be taken care of later in the week, or even later.

5. MINI-CASE

When Leslie arrived at work on Monday morning, she opened her e-mail. Box 4 contains the memo that Personnel Director Frances Williams has sent to Melissa Korn, a teacher at Leslie's school, notifying her that she has been placed on intensive assistance.

Box 4   Intensive Assistance Memo

To: Melissa Korn
From: Frances Williams, Director of Personnel BASD
Re: Intensive Assistance
Date: May 12

With this memorandum you are hereby notified that in order for you to remain employed by the Britton Area School District, you must enroll in the BASD intensive assistance program as stipulated in the teacher collective bargaining agreement and abide by all of the findings set therein. Failure to successfully complete this program will result in your termination at the end of this forthcoming school year.

cc: Ben Richards
Principal
Personnel file

Your Task

Does this memorandum effectively communicate its intended purpose? What are the procedures/policy your school district uses for intensive assistance plans?

6. MINI-CASE

Later that same afternoon Leslie met with her mentor—Ed Carver, principal of River View Middle School—to prepare for her new duties as principal. The files they discussed are listed here:

- standardized testing
- truancy and attendance
- health policies and procedures
- student discipline and court referrals
- inservice days
- board meetings
- fire drills and building inspections

Your Task

Sit down with your school principal and discuss these issues. Focus on school board policy and administrative rules, as well as state laws and city ordinances as they pertain to these items.

7. CASE STUDY

Leslie was feeling a little overwhelmed after Ed left her office. So, she decided to call her long-time friend, Robert Wiszkowski, for guidance. After commiserating for about half an hour and making some small talk, Robert asked Leslie about her new contract. She thought it was probably a standard contract for any new administrator. Robert was skeptical and suggested that she get advice from her state principal association with regard to contract language. This talk made Leslie nervous; she opened up her copy of the contract (see figure 1) and looked it over.

It is hereby agreed by both the Board of Education and the BASD (hereafter referred to as "the Board") and Ms. Leslie O'Connor (hereafter referred to as "the Principal") that the Board does hereby employ the Principal.

The Board and the Principal stipulate the following:

1. Term of Employment

Leslie O'Connor is hereby employed as Principal for the BASD for the period of August 1–July 1 for the next two academic years.

2. Certification

The Principal will provide accurate documentation of her state certification and commensurate degrees/education levels as provided by the State Department of Public Instruction.

3. Compensation

For services rendered per this agreement, the Board will compensate the Principal the annual sum of $56,000. Upon Board approval, this base salary may be increased for the second year of this term. In addition, based on recommendation from the district administrator of the BASD, the Principal may also receive a merit increase based on the format stipulated in the BASD administrator collective bargaining agreement.

4. Fringe Benefits

During the term of this agreement, the Principal will receive the following fringe benefits:

A. Vacation Days: Ten (10) days of vacation may be taken annually. All legal holidays are exempt from this language. Vacation days are not allowed to be taken during the week immediately prior to or immediately following the beginning or conclusion of the school year.

B. Sick Leave: The Principal is entitled to ten (10) paid sick leave days annually. This may accumulate to ninety (90) days.

C. Medical Insurance: The BASD will pay full rate for either individual or family coverage for hospital, surgical, major medical and dental based on the BASD administrator collective bargaining agreement policy. The BASD will also pay full premium.

D. Life Insurance: The BASD agrees to compensate full payment of group term life insurance in an amount equal to 1.5 times the Principal's salary.

E. Liability Insurance: The BASD will provide 100 percent of the Principal's liability insurance during the full term of the Principal's contract with the BASD.

F. Disability Insurance: The BASD agrees to pay the full disability insurance premium after the first 60 days of this contract and will provide a monthly benefit equal to 75 percent of the Principal's salary.

G. State Retirement System: The Board agrees to pay full amount to the state retirement system.

H. Memberships: The Board will pay up to $500 annually for professional membership in organizations appropriate to the Principal's position. This $500 may include transportation, fees for registration and materials, plus an additional $100 annually.

I. Mileage: The Board will compensate the administrator for use of her personal car for school-related work at a rate set by the State Department of Public Instruction, up to $200 annually.

J. Annual Physical: The Principal will be required to successfully complete an annual physical with a medical doctor agreed to by the BASD. The Board will pay 100 percent of these expenses.

K. Professional Course Work: The Board will pay 100 percent of the Principal's professional course work that is directly required for recertification. Board approval will be required for all additional compensation.

Figure 1. *Britton Area School District Principal Contract*

5. Responsibilities

The Principal agrees to perform at a professional level of competence and to complete the services, duties, and obligations required by the state and the rules and policies stipulated to by the BASD Board of Education.

The Principal agrees to devote full time to the duties and responsibilities agreed to herein and to not engage in any pursuit of any activity that would interfere with said contractual responsibilities. These responsibilities are stipulated in Board policy with regard to the Principal job description.

6. Board/Principal Relationship

A. Duties: The Board will stipulate and delegate responsibilities to the Principal through formal policy statements, the function of specifying the required actions and designing the detailed arrangements under which schools shall be operated.

B. Meeting Attendance: The Principal will attend monthly Board meetings and other such meetings at the request of the District Administrator and/or the Board of Education. Furthermore, the Principal will attend all administrative meetings as required of principals.

C. Performance Review and Evaluation: The district administrator will review the Principal's annual performance and provide a written evaluation report. The district administrator and Principal will meet at the beginning of the academic year to prepare goals and corresponding activities, and will meet again for a mid-term progress report, and for a final summative evaluation annually.

D. Termination of Contract: There are two general conditions whereupon termination of the Principal contract may occur. First, in such cases where it is mutually agreed on by the Principal and the Board of Education, termination of the contract is agreed.

Second, termination may be based on performance indicators. When just cause exists during the term of this contract, the Board may terminate the contract and immediately discharge the Principal from employment provided that the Principal has received prior notice in writing from the Board, indicating its intent and the alleged reason(s) for such discharge. Upon written request by the Principal—made within ten (10) days of receipt of said notice, a hearing shall be conducted with full regard to due process.

E. Contract Renewal/Nonrenewal: Renewal and nonrenewal of this agreement shall be governed by State Statute 144.19(2) and (3).

F. Professional Liability: The Board agrees herein that it shall defend, hold harmless, and indemnify the Principal from any and all demands, claims, suits, actions, and legal proceedings brought against the Principal as it relates to her official capacity as Principal and agent of the Board of Education, provided that the incident in question arose while the Principal was acting within her scope of employment and professional responsibilities and not in violation of criminal action.

This contract has been executed in the state and will be governed in accordance with state laws.

_____

Date

_____

Board President

_____

Board Clerk

_____

Principal

Figure 1. _Britton Area School District Principal Contract (continued)_

Your Task

Check with your state principal association about contract language that it would recommend for all new principals. You may want to ask questions about length of contracts, rollover of contracts, insurance/benefits, extra duties, and so on. Interview your school district director of human resources to learn about common language in administrator contracts. Follow up with a chat with your mentor. Finally, what are the strengths and weaknesses of Leslie's new contract? What changes would you make?

8. CASE STUDY   ⌐17

While Leslie was on the phone, Robert asked her for some advice, too.

He said, "Leslie, I was transferred within the district to the largest elementary school and had to deal with a difficult situation. Let me give you the background and the scenario."

Background

"My school is a K–5 building with 600 students. I have three or four sections of every grade. My staff is diverse—some are very traditional, while others are more at the cutting edge of pedagogy and curriculum development. Our district has eighteen public elementary schools and eight parochial schools. My teachers don't report back to school until after registration."

Scenario

He continued, "I am new to this school. The district has no policy regarding parent requests for teachers. In the past, the sending teachers made the class rosters/placements, and parents found out during August registration. The rosters were already set when I started the job, and the teachers had copies of their rosters."

"During the first morning of registration, six parents complained they didn't like where their children were placed. Three of the parents (all with fifth-graders) are quite adamant that they wanted Mrs. Fairbanks, because they felt she would thoroughly prepare their children for middle school with her high standards and expectations, while Mr. Smitten is too slack in his standards and focuses his time on building kids' self-esteem. My secretary told me that I am bound to get many more requests for the entire building with another two or three for Mrs. Fairbanks. One of the parents told me that she and other parents are considering sending their children to one of the parochial schools if they weren't satisfied with my response."

Robert then queried, "What would you do Leslie? What would you say to these parents? What kinds of things should I have considered? And, what were my options? Would you have one short-term solution and a separate long-term solution? How would you then respond to the teachers?

"Man, that's tough, Robert," Leslie replied. "I'll have to think about that. It's too complex to answer now."

"I hear you, Leslie," came Robert's response. "Let me make it even tougher. I had some future kindergarten parents ask if they could come observe the kindergarten teachers so they could make educated requests. Is that appropate?"

What Would You Do?

What are your options? What do you need to consider? What is your plan of action? Please write down what contacts you will make and the questions you will seek to get answered. Likewise, write down your options, the one you will choose, and why. Finally, describe what you will tell the teachers and what you will tell the parents.

Follow-up

Should parents be allowed to make classroom observations to make educated requests?

Your Task

Put yourself in Leslie's shoes. What advice would you give Robert? Answer the questions he posed to Leslie. Talk to your principal to see what process they use for parent requests to observe their potential future teachers.

9. MINI-CASE   ו-ו

The first day of school was well under way when Leslie was stopped in the hall by two mothers as she walked from the cafeteria to the gymnasium. The parents wanted Leslie to hold an all-school assembly with a gentleman espousing family values.

Leslie felt caught off guard. She told them that she didn't know how much money the school had budgeted for assemblies. Leslie then asked the parents if this speaker had any references. Both parents were truly put off by this last point. They indicated that they could serve as his reference as they had already seen him and highly recommended him. Furthermore, he was a good Christian man. Leslie finished the conversation by asking the parents for any literature on this speaker and saying she would look at the school budget.

Your Task

How would you have handled this situation? Check your school policy/procedures in scheduling and holding school assemblies. Who makes these decisions? How are references checked, if at all?

10. CASE STUDY   ו-ו

Bob Schmitz, head custodian, was waiting for Leslie to finish her conversation with the two parents. He told Leslie that she should follow him to the boiler room. When they arrived, they found three men standing around the old boiler, which had a large puddle of water under it.

Murphy McKenzey, coordinator of buildings and grounds, was the first to speak: "Well, Miss O'Connor, you've got a bit of a problem here. It seems like you've got a bum boiler."

The puddle already was looking bigger. "What can be done about it?" Leslie asked.

Murphy replied, "This should have been replaced about five years ago, but with the budget cuts and the failed referendums and all, it never got done."

Bob asked the question for Leslie: "So, what's the plan?"

Murphy looked at Leslie, "Well, most of the boiler is fine, but the tank has to be replaced. It's a one-day job, but we have to order a new drum."

Leslie was getting tired of she and Bob having to ask questions. It was like pulling teeth to get these guys to answer anything. "How long is that going to take?"

"Two to three weeks."

"What? Don't you have one in storage?"

One of the maintenance guys turned away and laughed. Ignoring him, Murphy went on, "If we had a spare one, it would have already been replacing this one."

"Can we limp along on this one until then?" Leslie asked.

"No way!" Murphy said. "Your water is not safe to drink!"

Leslie shot back, "What do you mean? We've had the drinking fountains on all day and have served hot lunch."

"That's okay, but now we have turned off the boiler."

"Are you telling me that we won't have safe water to drink and to use for lunch for the next two or three weeks?" Leslie asked in astonishment.

"That's right," Murphy said. "But don't worry. I have already ordered bottled drinking water. It will be here before school starts tomorrow. We'll have everything under control."

Leslie's head was spinning. On the one hand she was happy that the district had qualified workers in buildings and grounds—these guys knew what they were doing. But, on the other hand, this was going to be a huge headache.

"Aren't there any options?" Seeing no answer coming, Leslie said, "Well, do what you've got to do. I've got a letter to write to the parents and staff." (See box 5.)

Your Task

Rewrite the letter to reflect how you think this situation should be handled. Are there any options Leslie didn't consider with regard to shutting down the boiler for two to three weeks?

Box 6 contains the memorandum that Leslie prepared for her staff to announce that the school's water boiler was out of commission.

Your Task

Is this how you would have handled the situation? If you would have used a memo, how would you have written it? If you would not have written a memo to convey this information, what would you have done differently?

Box 5   Letter to Parents

Dear Families of Lancaster School,

Good afternoon. We discovered today that our very old school boiler has broken down. It will need to have a major component replaced. Unfortunately, it will take at least two weeks to purchase the replacement part. While this will be an inconvenience, we have everything under control.

Bottled water will be stationed throughout the building when your children arrive at school tomorrow morning. The toilets will remain in use as before. However, water for drinking and hygiene will have to be bottled. Therefore, please explain to your children that they can still use the toilets, but that they will have to use the bottled water to wash their hands in the restrooms and that they will have to use the bottled water to drink.

We have been assured by our Buildings and Grounds Department that there are no health problems. If you have any questions or concerns, please feel free to call me.

Sincerely,
Leslie O'Connor
Principal

Box 6   Memo to Lancaster Staff

To: Lancaster Staff
From: Leslie O'Connor, Principal
Re: Water Safety

Today we learned that our school boiler will need major repairs. Until the district is able to secure new parts, we will not be able to use our school water. This may take two or three weeks. We are sending a letter home to our parents today. Bottled water will be brought into the school tomorrow. While the toilets will remain operable, the drinking fountains and faucets will be shut off, so the children and staff will need to use the bottled water that will be positioned next to the fountains and faucets.

In advance, I thank you for your cooperation and understanding.

l ~ 24

11. CASE STUDY

When Leslie arrived back at her office, Georgine told her that Bill Harwell, education reporter for the newspaper, was waiting on the telephone to talk to her. Leslie hesitated to talk to the reporter. What was he going to ask? She didn't feel at all prepared. Besides, Tony Mousseli told her that district policy required all communications with the press to be handled through Bruce Lester, the coordinator of community relations for the BASD. But Leslie didn't want Mr. Harwell to feel as if she had anything to hide. What harm would it do to introduce herself and see what he wanted? She took the call in her office:

"Good afternoon, Mr. Harwell," Leslie began, trying to sound enthusiastic.

Bill Harwell introduced himself. "Welcome to Britton, Ms. O'Connor. I've been asked by my editor to write a brief article about you for our Community section. You know, introducing a new neighbor. Right now, I just have one question."

Thinking that one question couldn't hurt, Leslie replied, "Sure."

"What education experience do you have?"

"Well, I taught seventh-grade science the last five years in Brementon."

Bill Harwell continued, "You mean that you haven't been a principal before?"

Leslie felt her ears getting warm. "No, but I am certified as a principal and received my master's degree in educational administration."

"Very good, Ms. O'Connor. Thank you for your time."

Leslie felt relieved. "That wasn't too bad," she was thinking to herself, when the reporter interjected.

"Oh, one more thing, Leslie. Do you have any concerns about this school year?"

Since it was only one more question, Leslie felt comfortable answering it. "No, we have a great staff here with excellent families. I'm really excited about this school year. I guess my only concern is that we have a boiler on the fritz."

Bill Harwell continued, "I'm sure that you are, Leslie. But, are you aware of the fact that the Britton Area School District did poorly in the State Eighth Grade Reading Tests? In fact, they had only 51 percent of the students scoring at a proficient level. And your school was the worst of the three middle schools in the city."

Box 7   Newspaper Article

Everything's Great, Says Principal of Low-Ranking School

The newly hired principal of Lancaster Middle School, Leslie O'Connor, stated that she has a great school and staff even with the district's lowest scores on the recently released eighth-grade reading test scores. While O'Connor stated, "We have great teachers," she had no answer to the poor performance her school has had lately. Her biggest concern right now is the school boiler.

O'Connor has no experience as a school administrator. She has taught for five years and now is serving as the principal of Lancaster Middle School. We welcome her to the challenges that lie ahead.

Leslie realized that the reporter had just pulled a Lieutenant Columbo on her. "We have excellent teachers here," she said, "and I'm sure we will be addressing those issues this year."

"How do you know you have excellent teachers if this is your first year here, Ms. O'Connor?" Bill asked.

Thinking quickly, Leslie said, "The staff at Lancaster have an excellent reputation." With that, the interview concluded.

The article appeared in Saturday's issue of the local newspaper (see box 7).

Your Task ~schedule ask for appt. questions in advance~

Do you think Leslie handled the telephone interview inappropriately? If anything, what could she have done differently? Does your district have a policy stipulating interactions with the press?

1-24

12. CASE STUDY

Right after homeroom, sixth-grade home economics teacher Sandy Stone stepped into Leslie's office.

"Leslie, could you do me a favor? Peter, in my first period, fell asleep in class yesterday. This is the third time in these first two weeks of school. He just tells me he's tired but won't go into detail. I thought with your position of authority, you could talk to him, and he might open up."

Leslie tilted her head and shrugged her shoulders. "I don't know if I will be able to get anything more than you could, but I will give it a try."

Sandy went back to her room while Leslie got back to her mail. Within minutes Georgine brought Peter into her office.

"Good morning, Peter. Please have a seat," Leslie said as she motioned Peter to sit down across from her desk. "I understand that you've been very tired lately and that you've fallen asleep in class a couple of times. I'm concerned because then you don't have a chance to learn. What's the problem?"

Leslie was surprised to hear Peter start in right away: "I haven't been able to sleep very well lately."

Feeling like a guidance counselor, Leslie prodded some more. "Why not?"

"Lucy shakes my bed at night," Peter said.

Now Leslie felt more like a social worker. She felt as if this was not a topic she wanted to continue with. But, she did. "Who's Lucy?"

"Our six-foot pet boa constrictor. She sleeps with me and likes to move around at night."

"Oh my!" Leslie gulped. "That must be awful."

"She's not so bad, but Henry is. He's seven feet, and he has an attitude. My younger brother is really scared of him."

Leslie sent Peter back to his class and immediately called her school's social worker—Bob Phillips. She explained the situation to Bob and said she was not certain if this was something that was reportable. So, she'd let Bob decide. He thought it was worth looking into. He said he would visit the family later that morning and report back to Leslie before the end of the day.

Your Task

Do you think this issue is reportable? If so, who should have reported it (Leslie or Sandra) and to whom? If not, whom would you have turned to, or what would you have done differently? What are your district's policy and procedures for working with social services?

parents then -
Leslie, principal

13. MINI-CASE

During the past couple of weeks, Leslie has become frustrated with the discipline procedures at Lancaster. The problem, as Leslie sees it, is that all infractions are treated as equivalent as shown on the infraction ticket shown in figure 2. Because Leslie was so dissatisfied with the old discipline form, she created a new one (see figure 3).

Lancaster Middle School Discipline Ticket

Check one:

_____ First Offense (warning)

_____ Second Offense (15-minute detention)

_____ Third Offense (30-minute detention; phone call home)

_____ Fourth Offense (suspension)

Check one:

_____ running in the hall

_____ chewing gum

_____ swearing

_____ fighting

_____ homework not done; supplies not ready

_____ Other _____

Figure 2.   *Infraction Ticket—Current Version*

Lancaster Elementary School Discipline Ticket

Describe infraction: _____

_____

Describe disposition:_____

_____

Principal's signature

_____

Student's signature

_____

Figure 3.   *Infraction Ticket—New Version*

Your Task

Compare and contrast these two very different forms. Which do you like best and why? How should Leslie go about initiating this new infraction form with her staff and students? Write your own discipline ticket/form. Analyze the discipline ticket/form your school uses.

14. MINI-CASE

Before she was hired as principal, Leslie had promised herself that she would make teacher supervision and evaluation a top priority. She started drop-in visits during the third week of school. Her mentor and principal colleague, Ed Carver, showed Leslie the unofficial form he uses for impromptu visits. Leslie wasn't sure how much she liked it, but it was certainly better than nothing.

On the morning of September 21, Leslie did a drop-in observation of Sheryl Herlbutz's classroom. Figure 4 shows the form she completed from this mini-observation.

School: _Lancaster_   Teacher: _Sheryl Herlbutz_   Date: _9/21_

Subject: _Science_   Times: _10 minutes_

Topic(s): _Electricity_

Part of Class: Begin _____   Middle __X__   End _____   Transition _____

Student Grouping:

Whole Class __X__   Part Class _____   Small Group _____   Individual _____

Teacher Activities

Sheryl, you kept the students on task. You made sure all the students were working cooperatively on the experiment that was described in their learning packets. You asked questions of the whole class, periodically.

Student Activities

The children obviously enjoyed this lesson. They were glued to their experiments. They eagerly answered the questions you posed to them.

Comments

Keep up the great work! We're lucky to have you!

Teacher Signature   Principal Signature

_____   _____

Figure 4.   *Impromptu Classroom Observation*

Your Task

Your assignment is twofold. First, critique Leslie's feedback. While it is impossible for you to verify Leslie's findings, you can critique whether the form provides any valuable feedback to Sheryl. Is this more professional-growth oriented or more for accountability purposes? With that answer in mind, do you think this form/process served that purpose?

Your second task for this case is to create your own form for drop-in classroom observations. Keep in mind the purpose of these observations (professional growth or accountability). You might find it beneficial to visit with your school principal and review his or her approach to these types of visits.

15. CASE STUDY   2-28

On Tuesday morning, Leslie attended the monthly meeting for administrators in the district. After the four-hour meeting marathon, Leslie went to lunch with one of her new friends, Lisa Kelly. Lisa was also a new principal in the district, serving at Washington Elementary School. During their lunch conversation, Mrs. Kelly told Leslie of a problem she had and asked for her advice.

Background

Lisa said, "Washington Elementary, an inner-city school, has 250 students. Of these, 89 percent receive free or reduced lunch and 50 percent speak English as a second language. There are many dedicated teachers and staff here, and I consider this school to be a 'diamond in the rough.'"

Scenario

"I have been the new principal for nearly two months. One morning I was walking down the main hallway when a new, fairly elaborate wooden mural attracted my attention. The art teacher, whom I consider the best art teacher in the district, told me it would remain up for the next couple of months. The art teacher and the second-grade teacher have worked together on an insect unit, which is part of the mural. I noticed that the word *caterpillar* was spelled "caterpiller." Unfortunately, the letters were cut into the wooden mural and would have taken quite a bit of work to correct."

"I ignored the problem because I didn't want to embarrass this highly self-conscious teacher. Now I am feeling terrible. Did I do the right thing, Les?"

Your Task

If you were in Leslie's shoes, what advice would you give? Should you ignore the problem? Should you have the art teacher correct the problem? What are your options? What do you need to consider? What will you do?

16. CASE STUDY

After talking to Lisa about her situation, Leslie asked her for advice on a situation that she had dealt with the day before:

Background

The Pechard family had been going through an ugly marital dispute. The father is unemployed and has a drug history. The mother is on welfare. The sixth-grade boy, Frank Jr., attends your school.

Scenario

It was a Friday afternoon, ten minutes before the bell. Mrs. Pechard called Leslie, frantic. She explained that she and Frank Sr. had just had a huge argument. He had become extremely angry, thrown her against the wall, and left toward the school with a butcher knife. His final words were, "I'm getting Junior and taking him with me once and for all. And nobody's gonna stop me!" At that point, Leslie noticed that Junior had walked into the outer office with attendance papers.

Your Task

What do you do? Don't write down options. Write down your immediate instincts. Do this in two minutes or less.

Follow-up

What is your school or district policy on such issues?

17. IN-BASKET

Leslie spent all day Thursday and Friday attending a state conference for new principals. It was a great opportunity to network. A couple of the sectionals were great, especially the ones on school law and on administrative ethics. But, since Leslie was gone the last two days, she knew she would have a lot of work waiting for her back at the office. So, she went in to see what Georgine had placed in her in-basket (see box 8).

Your Task

Do the in-basket activities just as Leslie had to. Consider this school to be just like your school (or the school where you would like to work). These in-basket items are the mail and items you find waiting for you.

Use a separate piece of paper for each in-basket item. Respond to each item as you would in real life. For example, if you were to reply by writing a letter or an e-mail or a memorandum, actually write the letter or e-mail or memorandum. If you would put any items on a faculty meeting agenda, do that. If you were to make a telephone call, write down the issues, comments, questions you would cover. Identify each item as a priority 1, 2, or 3. Priority 1 is an emergency or urgent—an issue that you would handle today. A priority 2 is something you would handle on Monday. A priority 3 is something you would handle later in the week, or even later. You have one hour to complete this task.

Box 8   In-Basket

1. Memo
To: Leslie O'Connor, Principal Lancaster Middle School
From: Frances Williams, Director of Personnel BASD
Re: Grievance
Date: Friday

Leslie, as soon as you get this message, please get back to me. Your school librarian, Marion Kope, has filed a grievance against you. She is grieving the fact that you used her as a classroom substitute on Friday of last week when there were no subs available in the district.

I explained to her that you needed to fill C. J. Allen's classroom on Friday because there were no substitute teachers available that day. We needed to have a sub in that room. Marion is concerned that we feel the library is not as important as a regular classroom. Also, she does not want this to become a routine occurrence in the future. I told her that while this is not going to be routine, it is certainly within your responsibilities as the principal to do this. Still, we should talk soon.

2. E-mail
To: All Principals
From: Michelle Clark, District Technology Coordinator BASD
Re: Building Technology Misuse
Date: Friday
It has come to my attention that several of our schools are not following district policies when it comes to building web pages. Some schools are creating their own web pages without following district guidelines and format. Please review this policy 7114 and its corresponding administrative guidelines. Furthermore, we have been noticing that some employees are using district computers to send and receive personal e-mails. Not only is this wrong (see policy 7115), but it is also not appropriate for working hours. Please notify all of your staff of these policies.

3. E-mail
To: All Administrators
From: Vic D'Amasio

(continued)

Box 8 In-Basket (*continued*)

Re: Annual Administrator Bowling Game
Date: Friday
Heyo! It's that time again. It's time to sharpen your skills, and your skills—Peter. That's right. It's time for the 10th annual administrator bowling game. Now that the school year is well under way, we could use the chance to get out of the office early on a Friday afternoon.

We have the Britton Bowling Lanes reserved from 4 to 6 p.m. on Friday, October 12. Afterward, we will have burgers and beer and awards. R.S.V.P. by Monday. Be there or not.

4. Letter
Dear Principal,
We hope this letter finds you enjoying a wonderful school year. Because you have been such a good customer over the years, we would like to show our appreciation by giving you two free tickets to the Comedian Cutups. These tickets allow you and a friend or loved one to enjoy the show on October 23 with one complementary drink, each. With your hectic schedule, we know you could use a good laugh and a drink!

Again, we thank you for your business. We appreciate your continued support.

Sincerely,
Mike Yarling Jr.
Yarling Yearbooks

5. Handwritten Note
Dear Leslie,
One of our sixth-grade parents, Mrs. Patterson, has challenged a book in our library. The book is *Boilin' Trouble* by Sherry Herbeson. Mrs. Patterson claims that the book is inappropriate for young children because "it proclaims the benefits of witchcraft." Furthermore, she claims that the book is gory and scary and uses some inappropriate language. According to our district policy on challenged materials, you need to convene a meeting.

Sorry,
Marion Kope
Lancaster Middle School Library/Media Specialist

6. Handwritten Note

Dear Ms. O'Connor,

I can't believe it, but my husband has been transferred out of state. At our age, it will be impossible for him to find a different job with another company. So, we must take the transfer. We will be leaving in two weeks. Let me know what I can do to help you prepare for the transition.

Sincerely,
Georgine

7. Letter from a Parent

Dear Principal O'Connor,

On Tuesday, our daughter had her glasses broken at school. As her eighth-grade class was walking to gym class, two of the boys in front of her were horse-playing and shoving each other. Tim pushed Sam into our daughter and her glasses flew off her face and broke on the tile floor.

I want these glasses to be paid for. We replaced them last night at a cost of $123. The bill is attached. Furthermore, I want to know how these boys were punished.

Sincerely,
Mrs. Gail Petry
cc: Superintendent Mousseli

8. Letter from a Parent

Dear Mrs. O'Connor,

I apologize for writing this letter to you anonymously. However, I feel I need to do this because I don't want my child to get retaliated against. My child is in Ms. Korn's class. I have been concerned this year because of Ms. Korn's numerous absences. I have noticed that she has had substitutes on five occasions. Four of these times have been on Mondays. Rumors in the neighborhood say that she has been seen partying on Sunday nights and that she must have hangovers on Mondays. I think you should know about this. Several of us will be watching. If this does not change, we will contact the board of education.

Sincerely,
A concerned parent
(*continued*)

Box 8   In-Basket (*continued*)

9. Letter from Lawyer

Dear Principal O'Connor,

On Monday, September 7, our client—James Murphy—broke his elbow at Lancaster Middle School. James climbed up on a dirt bank (from the landscaping work that your school is doing) and played "king of the hill" with his classmates. He was pushed off the dirt hill and subsequently broke his right elbow. He is right-handed and may have permanent damage in that he may never regain full mobility.

We find that you and the Britton Area School District are negligent on two points. First, dirt should not be piled up and left on the playground. This is an attractive nuisance. Second, you and your school personnel did not provide sufficient supervision. Not only did teachers not tell the children to get off the dirt hill, but the children have never been told of any school policy about staying off of dirt banks.

This letter will serve as official documentation of legal proceedings. If you should have any questions, please call us at 555-9000.

Sincerely,
Frank Brohmer, Esq.

10. Handwritten Note from Custodian

Leslie,

I've had it with the graffiti that these kids are writing on the bathroom stalls. It happens every day. Ben always had me clean it up, and I did. It was not a big deal when the kids wrote in pencil, or even in pen. But now the swear words are being carved into the stalls. I'm tired of it. I spend way too much time with this problem, and it's getting to where I can't completely cover up the marks. Something needs to be done. Can you talk to the kids and monitor this more closely?

Thanks,
Bob Schmitz

11. Discipline Note from Antonio Black, Art Teacher

Leslie, I did not have time to find a discipline ticket, so I just wrote this down. I hope you don't mind. As I was teaching class, I noticed that some of the kids in the back of the room were giggling. I looked and saw that Michael Burns was holding up his middle finger—pointed toward me. He was trying to conceal it behind his book which he had on his desk top. When he noticed that I saw him, he looked guilty. I confronted him, but he denied it. But, I saw it, Leslie! I want him suspended!!

Thanks,
Antonio

12 Handwritten Note from Student
Misses Oconner,
Mr. Schmitz has been hanging around the bathrooms. Every time we go in their, he follows us in. This is scary. Please tell him to stop watching us go to the bathroom

Your students

13. E-mail from Parent
Dear Mrs. O'Connor,
This note must be held in complete confidence. I can't let my husband find out or he will go crazy, and I'm afraid what he might do. Yesterday, my son—Tommy—came home from school with a huge welt on his chest. According to Tommy he was goofing off in gym class. His teacher, Mr. Valders, took him into his office and started yelling at Tommy. Then he grabbed a hockey puck off of his desk and threw it at Tommy leaving the welt. I want Mr. Valders punished, but I don't want any word getting out about this.

Thank you,
Mrs. Harold Kanton

18. MINI-CASE   2-21-07 discussion

Leslie and her mentor went out to lunch at Los Diablos Mexican Restaurant. This was to be a working lunch, though, with Ed Carver. The plan was to talk about how Leslie was to be evaluated this year. The Britton Area School District used a version of management by objective (MBO). Ed showed Leslie the objectives he used his first year. They were pretty safe and standard. All principals were required to do between three and five objectives. One objective had to focus on curriculum. Ed advised Leslie to do another objective on "learning the ropes" about being a middle school principal. Another objective should probably focus on supervision and evaluation. Following are the three MBOs for Leslie's first year as principal at Lancaster Middle School. The format has been designed and adopted by the Britton Area School District.

Management Objective No. 1

Development of a Personal Management Philosophy and Style

I. Rationale

The Britton Area School District has a definite management philosophy and practices that have been incorporated into the administration of the district public schools. In order for the administrator to carry out the responsibilities of her position in the most competent and productive manner possible, she must have a thorough and complete working understanding of the Britton Area School District management philosophy, its accompanying practices, and its nuances.

II. Objective

The principal of Lancaster Middle School will begin to develop a clear and complete understanding of the Britton Area School District management philosophy and its accompanying practices. This process will be carried out through the remainder of this school year and will continue into the next school year. This process will encompass many areas, i.e., building scheduling, building budget construction, supervision and evaluation, cocurricular management, parent communication.

III. Expected Results

By the conclusion of this school year, the principal at Lancaster Middle School will have gained a foundational working knowledge of the Britton Area School District's management philosophy and accompanying practices. This foundational knowledge will include such areas as middle school philosophy and concept, middle school curriculum as it relates to each grade level and special programs, scheduling process, school budget construction.

The key emphasis will be placed on observation supervision and evaluation of staff members, both professional and classified.

IV. Operational Strategies

A. The principal will discuss the Britton Area School District's administrative handbook with her mentor administrator on a biweekly basis. Different sections of the handbook will be discussed at different intervals throughout the remainder of the school year. The initial meeting will take place in October.

B. The principal and her mentor will thoroughly discuss the organization and structure of the middle school as it relates to the Britton Area School District. The principal will take specific "hands-on" tasks to complete to assist her in reinforcing the information discussed, i.e., adjustment to school schedules (ongoing from October through June).

C. The principal will thoroughly discuss with her mentor major tasks that need to be accomplished at appropriate times during the remainder of the school year. The mentor will also provide the principal with "hands-on" activities related to these major tasks, i.e., the principal will be responsible for the construction of the entire budget as it relates to Lancaster Middle School. The principal will be responsible for the scheduling and the staffing process beginning with the projected enrollments for the next academic year and culminating in a completed staff and student schedule for said year.

D. The principal will be responsible, yet work directly with her mentor, for the observation, supervision, and evaluation process as it relates to the Britton Area School District. The observation data collected will then be reviewed together and discussed as to how it relates to the district evaluation process and be ongoing throughout the remainder of the school year.

E. The principal and her mentor will meet on a biweekly basis, at a minimum, to discuss school-related issues. The specific point of each meeting will be the orientation process as it relates to the principal. The principal will seek the advice of the mentor and keep the mentor abreast of pertinent decisions for the rest of the year.

F. The principal will meet monthly with the other middle school principals to share questions and concerns and to keep each other abreast of changes throughout each other's schools.

V. Responsibilities

The principal of Lancaster Middle School will be responsible for completing all the operational strategies above.

VI. Resources Needed

Throughout the course of the school year, various district personnel in the central office may be called on to elaborate on issues in areas discussed with the principal for her orientation process. Various monies may be requested for the principal to attend workshops in which she has indicated interest and which will enhance her performance at Lancaster Middle School.

VII. Miscellaneous

None

Management Objective No. 2

Supervision and Evaluation

I. Rationale

To ensure that Lancaster Middle School's students' needs are best being met through effective teaching, the Britton Area School District demands a high-quality supervision and evaluation program for its professional staff. This well-defined and structured supervision model developed by the district will continue to be implemented during the remainder of the school year.

II. Objective

The principal will develop a plan with her mentor for the implementation of this supervision model for the rest of this school year. This objective is to assist professional staff in growth with improvement of instruction and to provide for an excellent instructional program for students.

III. Expected Results

A. There will be an implementation of the supervision model for Lancaster Middle School during the remainder of the school year.

B. A systematic and consistent approach to supervision and evaluation will take place.

C. Teachers will fully understand the supervision and evaluation process in the building and in the district.

D. Teachers will better understand components of the supervision and the instructional process that go into effective teaching.

IV. Operational Strategies

A. The principal will review the teaching staff, noting their experience, past teaching evaluations within the building, and other pertinent data from the personnel files.

B. Staff will be informed about the process to be used in supervision and evaluation in our school. The principal will present these procedures at the faculty meetings and will outline the process to be used.

C. The principal will develop a plan of supervision and evaluation that will be submitted to the director of supervision services. This will outline the tentative schedule of supervision and evaluation of staff during the last semester of the school year.

D. Teachers who are new to the district, probationary teachers, or teachers for whom we have a concern will be evaluated at least three times before the end of the year.

E. If it is observed by the end of February that there are any teachers having difficulties and who may be candidates for nonrenewal or probationary status, the superintendent's office will be notified by March 1.

F. When outstanding teaching performances are observed, the principal will recognize the staff members involved.

G. Annual evaluations will be completed by May 15 and submitted to the director of personnel services. The principal will submit a written self-evaluation by May 20 to the superintendent and director of administrative services.

V. Responsibilities

A. The principal will be responsible for the overall supervision and evaluation process of this building. She will make sure that the model for the Britton Area School District will be followed and work effectively with other administrative staff members to iron out potential difficulties.

B. The central office administrative staff will be contacted periodically for consultation in the event of potential probationary or nonrenewal status for staff members.

VI. Resources Needed

Cooperation is needed from the department of personnel services to assist in identifying the status of staff. Support may be needed from the central offices as it could relate to potential staff status.

VII. Miscellaneous

None

Management Objective No. 3

Middle School Curriculum

I.   Rationale

When the administrator assumes a new position it is important that the administrator become knowledgeable about the curriculum and programs being taught within the building.

II.   Objective

The principal will become knowledgeable about the middle school curricular areas and special programs as well as related issues concerning students and staff in the building.

III. Expected Results

A. To become familiar with the philosophy of middle school education, 6–8.

B. To become familiar with the reading program as it relates to middle school students and teachers.

C. To become familiar with the math program as it relates to middle school students and teachers.

D. To become familiar with other curricular areas, i.e., outdoor education, physical education, art, music, and so on, as they relate to middle school students and staff.

E. To become familiar with issues affecting middle school education and their effects on students and teachers.

IV.   Operational Strategies

A. The principal will seek out middle administrators, her mentor, and teachers to discuss the intent and philosophy of middle school education as well as doing professional reading in the same area.

B. The principal will initiate contacts with central office curriculum coordinators in addition to the director of curriculum and instructional services as well as her mentor to gain knowledge and insight about math, reading, science, and other curricular areas.

C. The principal will schedule and host meetings for those teachers responsible for special programs, i.e., bilingual, ESL, LD, chapter I, and so on, to present information about their programs and answer questions about their programs for the faculty.

D. The principal will attend sixth-grade camp to become familiar with the outdoor education program.

E. The principal will become actively involved in discussions and decision making with teachers in the building as it pertains to middle school issues as they come to the forefront in the course of the school year.

V. Responsibilities

The principal is responsible for establishing a knowledge base of curricular offerings in the middle school setting and is the instructional leader in the building.

VI. Resources Needed

Cooperation is needed from the building faculty and other building administrators, central office coordinators, and the director of curriculum and instructional services to become familiar with the total middle school curriculum.

VII. Miscellaneous

None

Your Task

Critique the whole idea of management by objective. What are its strengths and weaknesses? Regarding the cases just presented, do you think that the MBOs will help Leslie be a more effective principal? Explain. What does your district require for its administrators? Use either your district guidelines or an MBO format to write a draft of your professional goals for your first year as an administrator.

2-21-07

19. CASE STUDY

On February 7, Sammi Smythe reported to Leslie that she had been sexually assaulted by an older boy in the school. Box 9 contains the Britton Area School District policy and administrative rule as it relates to students assaulting other students.

Box 9   Sexual Harassment Policy

Policy 420

Sexual harassment of students is a very serious issue and will be dealt with accordingly by the administration and board of education of the Britton Area School District. Student sexual harassment will not be tolerated in any fashion.

Sexual harassment includes any form of unwanted sexual advances or actions, purposeful or not purposeful, by one person on another person. Such advances include, but are not limited to, unwelcome or unwanted physical contact, requests or demands for sexual favors, verbal abuse, and display of sexually graphic or explicit materials. (Note: Other examples and further details of the policy will be found in Policy 420.1.) Because of the serious nature of student sexual harassment, the administration must rigorously follow the Administrative Rule 420.2 in dispensing with action of any complaint.

Administrative Rule 420.2
Sexual Harassment of Student

Pursuant to Policy 420, Sexual Harassment of Students, the Britton Area School District requires all administrators to rigorously follow these steps in handling all sexual harassment of students. Once a student, or parent of a student, complains of a sexual harassment incident to any teacher or administrator, the administrator will begin to document the action using form 420.3. In general, the procedures are as follows:

1. The administration will listen to the complainant and document his or her concerns. Subsequent to this informal meeting, the administration will discuss the issue with accused offender(s). Should the problem not be resolved at this step, the administration will move to step 2.

---

2. At this stage a formal complaint will be placed in writing under form 420.3. The complaint will include names of the aggrieved, the accused, date, time, location, and details of the complaint. The administrator investigating the complaint will immediately notify the director of human resources and file a report within ten calendar days of receiving the complaint. The report must include the administration's findings and the subsequent resolution. A copy of this report will be given to the person making the complaint, the accused, and the director of human resources.

3. If any of these aforementioned parties disagrees with the administration's findings or resolution, he or she must make a written appeal to the district administrator within ten calendar days. The district administrator will meet with all parties involved in the process to this point, separately, and make a recommendation for resolution. Such findings must be put in writing and presented to each of the aforementioned parties within ten calendar days.

4. Should either party of the aggrieved or accused disagree with the findings or resolution, she or he has ten calendar days to file a written complaint to the president of the Board of Education of the Britton Area School District. The BOE has ten days to complete its findings and report back to all parties.

5. If any party, aggrieved or accused, disagrees with the BOE's findings, he or she can then file a complaint with the State Department of Education.

Your Task

Review your district policy for sexual harassment and assaults of students. Talk to your building administrator and see how she or he would initiate the policy here. In other words, what would she or he do in this case? Share your response with your classmates. Also, Sammi did not complete a formal written complaint. What is Leslie's responsibility in this matter?

20. CASE STUDY

Georgine cleared her throat as she walked into Leslie's office, causing the rookie principal to glance up from her policy manual.

"You have a phone message from the Whitehursts, Miss O'Connor."

Leslie saw a chance to get away from pouring over that dry policy manual. So, she picked up her telephone and returned the call.

"Hello, Mrs. Whitehurst? This is Leslie O'Connor, principal at Nicholas' school."

"Oh, yes. I had hoped you would call when my husband is home after work, tonight. But I guess this is all right. Mr. Whitehurst and I are deeply troubled with the letter we received from your school this week. The school district continues to push their secular sex education program down our throats. This issue is a deeply personal and family matter. We wish you wouldn't teach this."

"I understand, Mrs. Whitehurst," Leslie replied. "And, you're right. This is a personal family matter, and you can remove your child from school that afternoon so that he won't have to watch the videos and participate in the discussion." This seemed quite reasonable to Leslie.

"I wish my husband were here. He is more direct and forceful. Our concern is that it will be unduly embarrassing to pull Nicholas out of school that day. In fact, it brings the whole issue to the front by doing this. We feel it is too early to teach children about these issues. But you force our hand. I wish you could understand our frustration!"

Leslie was at a loss for words. She never liked to teach sex education, anyway, and Mrs. Whitehurst seemed to make a valid point. She responded thoughtfully, "I really don't know what to say, Mrs. Whitehurst. I do understand your point, and I think it's valid. This is district policy, though—"

Mrs. Whitehurst interrupted, "You mean you have no power as a principal to take care of this? Are you saying I should go over your head to the board of education?"

"I think it is important that you share your ideas and concerns with the board. That's how they make their decisions. I'm sorry I can't be of more help."

"I'm sorry, too. We'd send Nicholas to a parochial school if we could. Public schools get me so upset at times."

With that the phone conversation was over. It seemed as if it took thirty minutes, but it was only six minutes long. Leslie was worried about Mrs. Whitehurst. Leslie knew that she would be calling board members and Leslie wanted to give Tony Mousseli a heads-up. She called the superintendent's office but had to leave a message.

Your Task

Does Mrs. Whitehurst have a point that is worth considering? What do your principal and district do for such cases? Is the opt-out option the best choice we can come up with?

21. CASE STUDY

While Leslie had routinely attended school board meetings since she was an interim principal, this meeting had a special significance for her. Mr. and Mrs. Whitehurst were in attendance and spoke of their concerns regarding the human growth and development curriculum pursued by the Britton Area School District. What follows is the agenda for that meeting.

Britton Area School District Board of Education

Meeting Agenda
February

I.   Open meeting notification pursuant to SS 20.21(3)
II.   Pledge of Allegiance
III. Agenda-Related Public Forum
IV.   Consent Resolution Items
    A. Minutes of previous Board of Education meeting
    B. Bills Payable
    C. Personnel
       i.   Appointments, changes in contracts, retirements
       ii. Resignations
       iii. Unpaid leaves of absence
    D. Zoning change request
    E. Minor line-item budget change requests
    F. Minor building and maintenance change requests
V.   Individual Resolution Items
VI.   Board and Administrative Reports
    A. Report of the Superintendent
    B. Reports of Committees

VII. Board of Education Workshop
    A. Budget for next school year
    B. Standardized test results
VIII. Non-Agenda-Related Public Forum
IX.   Adjourn to Executive Session
    A. Consideration of the employment, promotion, compensation, or performance evaluation data of public employees pursuant to SS 20.46(1)(d)
X.   Adjourn

Your Task

Attend a school board meeting of your local school district. Talk to your superintendent about the agenda. Spend some time talking not only about items on the agenda, but also about formal procedures of board meetings and the politics of open public meetings, as well as work "behind the scenes" in preparation for these meetings. Also, ask about when the board can meet in closed session and to what degree board members can meet outside of formal meetings. Then, discuss your findings with your classmates.

22. CASE STUDY

Parent Jean Verboud was upset about a book titled *A Child Called "It,"* which her sixth-grade child brought home. She demanded that Leslie pull it off the library shelves. Leslie told her that she would initiate the district protocol for challenged materials. Box 10 shows the district policy and checklist for such challenged materials. The formal written complaint filed by Jean Verboud is shown in box 11.

Your Task

Go back to your district and review its policy and procedures for challenged library materials. Then, actually go through the process of responding to this challenge using the query by Ms. Verboud. You might choose to do this in class by creating a committee to address the issue.

Box 10   Procedures for Reconsideration of Instructional Materials

Policy 344
Administrative Rule
Procedures for Reconsideration of Instructional Materials

This policy, administrative rule, and forms must be used should a parent or citizen complain or wish to have a book or other media removed from one of the BASD's library/media centers.

I. Library/Media Materials
   A. Listen to the person challenging the school's materials. Explain to him or her the formal procedures for challenging said materials. Provide for him or her the challenged materials form (344.A).
   B. Temporarily remove the challenged item(s) from the shelves until such time as the building-level review committee (which must include the principal, library/media specialist, and two teachers) has had the opportunity to review the challenge and make a decision.
   C. Inform the district Coordinator of Library/Media Services, the Director of Curriculum and Instruction, and the Superintendent of the challenge.
   D. Convene the building-level review committee to:
      1. Examine all materials.
      2. Review general acceptance of the material by using standard sources for such reviews.
      3. Weigh values and form opinions based on the material as a whole as opposed to singular passages taken out of context.
      4. Determine the disposition of the complaint as one of the following:
         a. Material should be withdrawn
         b. Material should be retained on the shelves
         c. Material should be retained with restrictions
      5. Share the building-level review committee's decision with the person challenging the district.
      6. Provide copies of the report to the person challenging the materials, to the principal, to the district Coordinator of Library/Media Services, to the Director of Curriculum and Instruction, and to the Superintendent.

(continued)

Box 10   Procedures for Reconsideration of Instructional Materials (*continued*)

E. If the person challenging the materials is not satisfied with the review committee's decision, she or he is invited to appeal that decision to the Director of Curriculum and Instruction who will convene a new review committee made up of the district Coordinator of Library/Media Services, the Superintendent (or designee), the library/media specialists from within the district, and other staff as appropriate. The committee must:

1. Follow procedures (4)(a) through (e) above and prepare a report within ten school days.
2. Send a copy of the report to the person making the challenge, the principal of that school, and to the superintendent.
3. If after step 5 the decision remains unacceptable, the person making the challenge may appeal to the Superintendent within ten school days. The Superintendent will:
   a. Schedule a meeting within five school days with the person making the challenge.
   b. Issue a decision within ten school days following that meeting.

Box   11   Parent   Request   for   Reconsideration   of Library/Media Materials

Type of Material: library book
Author: Dave Pelzer
Title: *A Child Called "It"*
Challenged by: Jean Verboud

Please answer the following questions. Attach additional sheets if needed.

1. Specifically, why are you challenging this material? (Please list page numbers)
   This book is very disturbing. Its depictions of abuse and neglect are gruesome and horrific. Our children should not see this book. It's too disturbing!

On pg. 41—"Gripping my arm, Mother held it in the orange-blue flame. My skin seemed to explode from the heat. I could smell the scorched hairs from my burnt arm. . . ."

On pg. 55—" . . . she brought out one of Russell's soiled diapers. She smeared the diaper on my face."

On pg. 87—"Out of the corner of my eye I saw a blurred object fly from her [my Mother's] hand. A sharp pain erupted from just above my stomach. I tried to remain standing, but my legs gave out, and my world turned black."

2. Did you read the material in its entirety? If not, what parts did you read?

   Yes

3. What do you think might be the result of children reading this material?

   Simply their emotional psyche. This would be very disturbing to youngsters. They are not ready to read such materials and could be emotionally scarred. They could become very depressed and have nightmares.

4. Is there any age group for which you would recommend this material?

   No sooner than high school.

5. Have you had the opportunity to read any published reviews of this material? If not, we will provide you with such materials.

   No, I haven't seen any reviews. I would be happy to see some.

6. In its place, what material would you recommend to convey the same information?

   I don't think any materials have to replace it.

7. What would you like your school to do with the material you challenged?

   _X_ Do not assign it to my child for any assignments.

   _X_ Remove from the library/media center.

   ____ Withhold it from my child if available in the media center or classroom.

   _X_ Send it back to the school library/media center for re-evaluation.

   ____ Offer alternative instruction or content to my child.

   _X_ Invite me to share my concerns with the library/media center review committee.

Parent Signature _Jean Verboud_ Date _____

23. CASE STUDY

As Leslie was walking back to her office after observing a teacher's classroom, Georgine met her in the hall. This was Georgine's last day. Leslie thought the older, tall gentleman in a blue pinstriped suit standing next to her might be her husband.

"This is Miss O'Connor," Georgine said, looking at the man and pointing at Leslie.

The man reached into his suit coat pocket and handed Leslie an envelope. "Ms. O'Connor, this is for you." With that the man turned on his heel and left the building.

Leslie was subpoenaed for court with regard to the matter of Franklin McCormick's habitual truancy problems. This case was initiated by former principal Ben Richards. Franklin is now a seventh-grade student.

A copy of the district policy and form can be found in box 12.

Your Task

Compare your school district's policy and process/forms for student attendance and truancy. Likewise, review your state laws in these matters. Then, as an actual case begins at your school, take the time to go through this process.

24. CASE STUDY

Mrs. Allison Birnbaum had scheduled this morning's meeting with Leslie as soon as Thanksgiving break was over. Leslie sipped on her cup of very hot tea in the tastefully furnished living room of the Birnbaums.

In a serious yet diplomatic tone, Mrs. Birnbaum began, "Leslie, I really appreciate you taking the time out of your busy schedule to meet with me this morning. The concern that my family and I have is very important to us, and I know that I speak for a few other families."

Leslie knew the topic in general, but did not understand what the specific concerns would be. "I'm always happy to meet with you, Allison."

Box 12   Student Attendance and Truancy

Policy 420
Administrative Rule

I. RULE: According to State Statute 120.15, a student younger than 18 will be considered an habitual truant as a result of missing part or all of any ten school days (unexcused) in a given semester. The school district must create and maintain a policy to meet SS 120.16 standards.

II. PROCEDURES for the Britton Area School District:

A. When a child misses part or all of five school days, the school will send a certified letter to the parents of said child. This letter will explain State Statutes 120.15 and 120.16 as well as district policy 420. With this same communication, the student and family will be notified of district procedures initiated upon the student being deemed an habitual truant.

B. Once a child has been deemed an habitual truant, the school principal or designated attendance officer will schedule a truancy referral meeting with the parents of the child. The purpose of this meeting will be to explain to the parents that a truancy referral has been initiated and to discuss ways to ameliorate the truancy.

C. Concurrently, the principal or designated attendance officer will initiate a "truancy referral." This referral must include the following:

1. Building Consultation Team (BCT) meeting. Members will try to determine whether modifications in the student's in-class or out-of-class program can be made, or if special education programming is appropriate.

2. Guidance Counselor appointment. The school guidance counselor will meet with the child to determine whether the child might have other nonacademic issues affecting school attendance.

3. Principal or designated attendance officer meeting. The principal or said designee will meet with the child to determine whether any external behavior problems might be affecting the child's school attendance.

4. The school social worker and principal or designated attendance officer will then meet to review the findings from points 1 to 3.

5. The school social worker will then take this truancy referral to the county clerk of courts to be turned over to the county district attorney.

"My family is Jewish. And there are so many things that happen in our public schools and in the community that are Christian in nature. It's difficult to raise our children in their heritage when so many Christian events are always taking place. Our children always feel left out and are uncomfortable."

"What kinds of things at Lancaster are you talking about?" Leslie queried.

"Well, we already get off for 'Christmas Break' and for 'Easter Vacation.' But even leading up to those Christian holidays, there are things going on in the school that are purely sectarian. For example, the teachers have the kids making ornaments, doing gifts, preparing Christmas cards and things to hang in the hallways. The biggest issue of all is the Christmas concert. For weeks our children are required to practice Christian songs and then asked to perform for their families one evening."

"Your children don't have to participate, Allison," Leslie replied. Then, remembering her conversation with Mrs. Whitehurst, she realized how hollow those words must sound.

"I'm sorry," Leslie continued. "That isn't much comfort, is it?"

"No, it's not. But I'm glad you realize that. We're not asking that the school do away with the Christmas concert. We're asking, though, that the focus change from Christianity to religions or ethnicities around the world—in our community for that matter. In other words, can't the school have the kids sing all kinds of songs, not just Christian songs?"

"That makes a lot of sense," Leslie said with a smile.

"I know it does, but I've had this conversation with Ben Richards the past three years," Allison commiserated. "Ben agreed with me, but he couldn't get the music teacher and the rest of the staff to agree. He said the teachers always told him about their traditions!"

Leslie didn't know what to say, but she was certainly frustrated. "I completely agree with your position, Allison. I feel so strongly about this that I will make the decision as the principal. We are going to make some necessary changes."

Leslie and Allison finished their tea as they talked about a variety of topics. Leslie wasn't sure how she was going to handle this situation, but she promised herself that she wouldn't back down.

Your Task

Did Leslie do the right thing by standing up for her values and making a promise to Allison? What would you say in this conversation? Does your school have any policy for taking into account Christmas concerts and how they might impact people from different backgrounds? Explain.

25. CASE STUDY

Now that winter break was over, Leslie got busy focusing on next year's school budget. She did not like the idea of the principal arbitrarily setting aside particular amounts of money for each teacher and department. This seemed too artificial and based more on history and past practice rather than need. She decided to go with a form of zero-based budgeting. To do this, however, she would need to educate the staff about the state accounting system, how money was allocated to each school, and how much money was spent in each department the past couple of years. In this way, the staff would truly understand the budget and could make wise decisions as they made next year's budget.

Leslie made a set of transparencies of the budget that she showed her faculty. Two years ago, there were 528 students at Lancaster Middle School; last year, there were 552 students. The projected enrollment for next year is 560 students. Figure 5 shows a sample budget for the school.

Your Task

Compare the sample budget in figure 5 with your school's budget. Examine the budget from the past two years. What items never change? What items have major discrepancies? Why? How is your budget put together? Are the teachers told how much they are allotted, or do you use some version of zero-based budgeting?

26. IN-BASKETS

Things had begun to pile up on Leslie, so she decided to go into work on this cold Saturday morning in January. With a long, deep breath,

Account No.	Account Description	2 years ago	last year	proposed
10-213-325-110000	Repairs	$4,200	$3,625	
10-213-410-110000	Supplies			
	(general ed.)	13,160	13,400	
10-213-410-120000	Dues and fees	500	500	
10-213-411-120000	Copy machine rep.	400	400	
10-213-551-110000	Equipment	4,858	5,300	
10-213-999-110000	Miscellaneous	1,528	2,052	
10-213-410-121000	Art supplies	3,140	3,260	
10-213-410-122000	English supplies	750	750	
10-213-470-122000	English textbooks	2400	2400	
10-213-410-123000	Foreign language			
	supplies	500	750	
10-213-410-124000	Math supplies	1,056	1,104	
10-213-412-124000	Math workbooks	1,000	-0-	
10-213-313-125000	Music supplies	660	690	
10-213-313-125000	Music repairs	300	300	
10-213-410-126000	Science supplies	1,056	1,104	
10-213-470-126000	Science textbooks	-0-	500	
10-213-410-127000	Social studies			
	supplies	300	300	
10-213-470-127000	Social studies			
	textbooks	-0-	1,200	
10-213-410-135000	Home ec. supplies	2,500	2,500	
10-213-410-136000	Tech. ed. supplies	3,000	3,000	
10-213-410-143000	P.E. supplies	660	2,067	
10-213-410-213000	Guidance supplies	650	650	
10-213-410-214000	Nursing supplies	1,410	750	
10-213-410-241000	Principal supplies	4,600	4,450	
10-213-341-256000	Student transportation	3,050	3,600	
10-213-341-162000	Student trans.			
	(athletics)	2,000	1,800	
10-213-410-162000	Athletic supplies	450	400	
10-213-434-222200	Periodicals	1,584	1,656	
10-213-431-222200	Media	5,280	5,520	
10-213-435-222000	Media software	500	500	
Total Budget		**$61,492**	**$64,528**	**$65,000**

Figure 5. Sample Budget

Leslie turned to the pile of messages and notes (see box 13) that she was unable to get to the day before.

27. MINI-CASE

Leslie had just finished scolding a boy for acting like a fool in the hallway when her office phone rang. She knew this had to be another ad-

Box 13   In-Basket

1. Phone Message
Anonymous caller complaining about lunch lady walking to school yesterday, obviously drunk.

2. Letter
Dear Principal O'Connor,
Our twins (Jackie and Jordan) have Ms. Jones for sixth-grade Social Studies. Jackie has always been a straight-A student. Jordan has worked hard to overcome his disability and has always earned straight A's, as well. As a point of clarification, Jordan received LD support at school.

At midterm, Ms. Jones sent home progress reports for all of her students. She indicated that both Jackie and Jordan were receiving straight A's. In fact, as unlikely as it seems, they both had identical percentages in nearly all their subjects. No homework was missing. As you can imagine, we were much dismayed and concerned when the twins brought home their report cards this evening and the grades were different. Their scores/percentages remained in the A range and stayed equal to each other. While Jackie had straight A's on her report card, Jordan had straight B's—even though the percentages were the same. On the bottom, Ms. Jones wrote something to the effect that because Jordan received LD support, he could not receive A's in those subject areas where he gets help.

How can this be!? We would like to meet with you to resolve this issue. Please reply to us at your earliest convenience. Jordan cried himself to sleep tonight.

Sincerely,
Mr. and Mrs. Dutweiler

3. Phone Message
Please return phone call from Mr. Wilton Leduce. He's the store owner of Leduce's Market, down the street from school. He's complaining about our kids hanging around his store before and after school and causing problems.

4. Handwritten Note from a Seventh-Grader
Deer Principle,
The lunch lady Mrs. Carlson swoar at us on the playground today. She said we should keep our beeping mouths shut. A bunch of us

(continued)

Box 13 In-Basket (*continued*)

were their. My mom says its because she is a drunk. Please stop her being so mean to us.

Your friend,
Victor

5. Handwritten Note from Guidance Counselor

Hi, Leslie. I would like for you to permit me to attend the national conference for AODA counselors in Las Vegas next month. I won't need a sub. I already have permission from downtown. They're paying for my transportation and hotel. But they said you would need to pay the $200 registration fee and give me permission.

Thanks in advance,
Dave Phlander

6. E-mail Memo from Superintendent

To: Leslie O'Connor, Principal at Lancaster Middle School
From: Tony Mousseli, Superintendent of BASD
Re: Community Service
Date: December 19

The Tri-City Parents of the Handicapped Support Network (a not-for-profit organization) has asked me to identify a member of our administrative team who could lead them in a strategic planning workshop. The BASD Administrative Team has a tradition of volunteering to support community service groups. I recall from our interview that you have been part of strategic planning in your former school district. I am requesting that you provide service to this worthwhile group. They would like you to lead them in a one-day workshop to help them define their board roles and then to start the strategic planning session. Please call Vernon Franklin of the Tri-City PHN to arrange for this opportunity, or call me if you have any questions.

7. E-mail from Sixth-Grade Teacher of Math

Leslie, I would like to attend the national AODA conference in Las Vegas. It is my intention to start serving as a group facilitator this year.

Thank you,
Heidi

8. E-mail from One of Leslie's Former Professors
Good afternoon, Leslie,
I would like to invite you to be a guest speaker in my Tuesday night class in two weeks. This is my Principal Internship course, and I'd like to have you talk of your first-year experiences. You'd be great! What do you think?

Most sincerely,
Lee Palm, Ph.D.

9. Handwritten Note from Student
Hi, Mrs. O'Connor
I'm in Mrs. Herlbutz Science class. We're doing a unit on insects, and I'd like to bring in my pet scorpion and pet tarantula. Mrs. Herlbutz said she doesn't mind, but I need to get your permission. Will you give me permission?

Thank you,
Billy Xiong

10. Letter from Parent
Dear Ms. O'Connor,
Our family has a great opportunity to travel to China; I will be making a speech in Beijing. We will be leaving this coming Thursday and will be returning in two weeks. Would you be so kind as to have Andy and Susie's teachers get their assignments around so they can work on their homework at night at the hotel.

Sincerely,
Herb Price, Ph.D.

11. Handwritten Note
Hi, Leslie
Sheryl H. lost her pet python. She tells me it's not poisonous. But since her room is next to your office, I thought I'd let you know. I looked for about two hours and could not find it.

Good luck,
Bob Schmitz

12. Letter from Student Council
Dear Principal O'Connor,
Due to all the hatred, anger, and terrorism in this world, a number of the Lancaster Student Council would like to start a prayer group

(continued)

Box 13   In-Basket (*continued*)

on Mondays, Wednesdays, and Fridays during the lunch hour. Our Student Council advisor, Mrs. Humphries, has said she will allow us to use her music room during this time. All students and teachers can attend these informal meetings, but nobody will be required, or even asked, to attend. We would like to ask for your approval.

Sincerely,
Katie Humphries
Student Council President

13. Note from Teacher Aide
Dear Ms. O'Connor,
Something has me very troubled today. I noticed that Tommy Gea had a strange T-shirt on this morning. When I looked closer, I noticed that it said, "Rah, Rah Ree, Kick 'em in the knee. Rah, Rah Rass, Kick 'em in the other knee." I know that this wasn't direct swearing, but it was obvious. Kids were laughing about it.

I told Tommy to go home and change the shirt. He said he lived too far away. I told him to have his mom bring a new shirt to school. He said she was out of town for the day. He has no other family. So, I told him to turn the shirt inside out. He raised a ruckus, but did it. Can you talk to him?

Thanks,
Olive Patterson

ministrator from within the district, because no one else knew her direct number. Indeed it was.

"Good morning, Leslie. This is Frances."

"Good morning to you, too, Frances," Leslie replied, wondering what the director of personnel wanted.

"We've got to get together sometime this morning and talk about posting Georgine's job, setting up interview protocol, and scheduling the interviews."

"I'm on my way," came Leslie's response. She had never done this before and was looking forward to the experience.

Frances told Leslie to create a job posting for Georgine's job. The posting is shown in figure 6.

Britton Area School District Job Opening
Position: Lead Building Secretary
Location: Lancaster Middle School
Application Deadline: April 15

The Britton Area School District is looking for applicants for a full-time, eleven-month lead secretary at Lancaster Middle School. The position is open immediately and will remain open until filled.

This secretary is broadly responsible in supporting the work of the building principal and assistant principal. The successful candidate works directly with staff, students, and parents. Furthermore, this secretary is responsible for account maintenance, billing, filing, correspondence, and other traditional secretarial duties. Candidates must be personable, computer-literate, and well-organized, and have bookkeeping knowledge.

Hours are from 7:30 a.m. to 4 p.m., Monday through Friday. Starting pay is $11.35 per hour with very good fringe benefits.

Figure 6. *Job Posting*

Your Task

Meet with your director of personnel or human resources and learn (a) the procedures for posting a position and screening applicants' files, (b) interview protocol, and (c) final approval processes. If you're fortunate, your principal will allow you to be a part of the process of hiring new people henceforth.

28. CASE STUDY

Vernon Franklin, executive director of the Tri-City Parents of the Handicapped Support Network, and Elizabeth Quiggley, board president of Tri-City, met Leslie for lunch at the Le Croix Bistro. The purpose of this working lunch was to plan for the next week's strategic planning workshop.

"It's a true pleasure to meet you, Leslie," Elizabeth said quickly. Elizabeth was a tall, elegant woman. She carried herself with a clear air of professionalism and a feeling of urgency. "We are in need of your expertise, and I'm thrilled to have you on board. Shall we get started?" she asked.

Leslie felt as if she should be intimidated by Mrs. Quiggley, but she was more in awe of her dedication to her cause than of her impressive presence.

After ordering their lunch specials, Leslie began, "Elizabeth and Vernon, could you describe for me why your organization exists."

Vernon looked toward Elizabeth and gave her a nod as if to say, "You can answer this one better than I."

Elizabeth looked at the table, took a long breath, and paused for what seemed like an eternity. Then after an agonizing minute, she started in a quiet tone. "My youngest son was born with a variety of physical impairments. He was always developmentally behind other children his age. While he eventually learned to walk, he was confined to a wheelchair by the time he was seven years old. He continued to get worse and has been bedridden ever since. Because of his physical handicaps, if you will, he was unable to attend school and is not as far along academically as he should be. He is now a teenager and is too big for me to handle physically. He is so frustrated and gets to be quite difficult at times.

"My husband and I and our two other children also have frustrations and at times have overwhelming stress. We thought there must be other people in our community who have similar stories and problems. You know, agony loves company. Anyway, we could not find any formal assistance out there. So we decided not to wait for something to help us, but decided to start our own organization. That's why we started Tri-City Parents of the Handicapped Support Network. Its primary goal is to provide support and comfort to parents and family members of handicapped kids. We know this is broad, but we thought by just getting started, direction would come from the needs of the families.

"That is our brief background," Elizabeth said. "We now need direction."

"I'm sorry for your difficulties and frustrations, Elizabeth," Leslie said. "What is the current status and needs of Tri-City PHSN?"

"Vernon, why don't you handle this one?" Elizabeth said.

"Well, our organization is less than a year old," Vernon said. "We have created our by-laws, which are very sound. Our problem is us. We have anywhere between five and nine people on our board of directors. Nine is the number we formally have in the by-laws, but we have never had all nine people there. In fact, we average about six or seven board members, but we have five core members who are always there and have been there from the beginning.

"Elizabeth and I aren't sure some of the board members should even be on the board. They might not have the gut desire to be on it, or they might not have the skills needed. So, I think what we need from you is help in delineating board roles and then in facilitating our strategic planning. I know you have done this, and I trust the business-approach you'll take. So, what do you think?"

Leslie knew she would do this, but had some other questions. "Can you tell me a little bit about the people on your board? Also, do you have any employees or is it all volunteer help?"

Elizabeth smiled. "Most of our members are parents of handicapped children, all different kinds of handicaps. Perhaps we're too eclectic, but I think that is part of what makes us special. Anyway, they're a good group but have little board-type experience. We have a few businesspeople on the board. One's a CEO, one is an attorney, one is a small-business owner, and one is your special education director in town. In my opinion, they are just as much of an issue on our board as the parents who have no board experience. At least the parents care very deeply and are committed. In my estimation, some of the 'professionals' are on the board either to pad their resumes or because their bosses told them to be on it. I know I sound cynical, but I want to get somewhere with this and we're at the point of spinning our wheels."

The three finished their meals. Leslie talked about how she envisioned the workshop unfolding, and Vernon and Elizabeth provided more detail about the board and some of the activities of the organization. They agreed to do the workshop on the Saturday after next.

Your Task

Figure 7 shows a series of documents that Leslie prepared for this strategic planning workshop. The documents include the agenda for all members; PowerPoint slides defining strategic planning, mission, vision, board roles, and responsibilities; and the actual action-plan matrix.

Your Task

You have just perused a series of documents. Take a close look at these and analyze them. Do you have the same definitions of vision and mission? Have you gone through strategic planning before? If so, how was it organized differently and similarly? Where do you agree

Strategic Planning and Board of Directors' Roles

Retreat Agenda

9:00–9:15 Introduction of the day
  • Know the Board of Directors' roles and functions
  • Begin to develop a strategic plan
9:15–10:00 The roles and functions of the Board of Directors
  • Presentation
  • Dialogue/Activity
10:00–10:30 Current status of the organization and any looming critical issues in the
           organization or community—presented by executive director
10:30–10:45 Break
10:45–11:15 Organization's Mission
  • Purpose of mission
  • Review current mission statement (rewrite as necessary)
11:15–11:45 Organization's Vision
  • Purpose of vision
  • Dialogue/Activity
11:45–12:30 Strategic planning preparation
  • Presentation—purpose
  • Identify strategies—through dialogue
12:30–1:30 Working Lunch
  • Think of strategies (subcommittees you'd like to be on)
1:30–3:00 Strategic Planning Process
  • Presentation—process
  • Members break into groups to begin developing strategies
3:00–3:30 Wrap-up
  • Groups report back to full group
  • Where do we go from here?

PowerPoint Slides

Strategic Planning

  • Strategic planning is the means by which the organization constantly recreates
    itself to achieve a common purpose.
  • It is an opportunity to define the changing needs of the clients and to restructure
    the organization to meet those needs.
  • The action plan is the explicit portion of a given strategy that outlines the tasks
    required to implement that program, the persons responsible for each task, the due
    dates (timelines) for each task, and possibly an analysis of the costs and benefits
    for the plan.

Mission

  • A broad statement of the unique purpose for which the organization exists and the
    specific function it performs
  • Mission is where we want to be now.

Vision

  • Where we want to be in five to ten years

Figure 7. *Strategic Planning Workshop Documents*

Board Roles

- The Board is responsible to its mission and for its successful implementation.
- To do this, it has three major functions or responsibilities:
  1. Strategic planning
     a. promoting and revising its mission (ongoing and routine)
     b. setting vision
     c. setting strategies (approaches to achieve the mission)
  2. Management of the CEO
     a. selection and retention
     b. professional development
     c. evaluation
     d. compensation
     e. termination
  3. Management of the Board itself
     a. focus—role definition
     b. membership
     c. structure and bylaws
     d. evaluate meetings

Board's Responsibilities

- Boards don't get involved in details—they don't have the expertise or time to do this.
- Boards don't get involved in the daily operations—they hire the CEO and staff for this.
- Boards aren't reactive, they are proactive.

Three Major Board Committees

1. Strategic Planning
   - Learn how to do strategic planning.
   - Keep current of issues/trends that affect the organization/mission.
   - Create subcommittees for each action plan.
2. Management of the CEO
   - Define CEO responsibilities and board expectations of CEO
   - Communicate with and evaluate CEO based upon CEO responsibilities/board expectations
   - CEO professional development
   - CEO compensation
3. Management of the Board itself
   - Identify and orient board members.
   - Determine nature of committee responsibilities.

Special Notes:

1. The executive committee is responsible for putting the agenda together. They make sure only appropriate items get put on the agenda. The meetings need to stay focused.
2. Other committees might include fund acquisition and accounting, marketing, buildings and grounds, policy development and review, and so on.

Figure 7.   *Strategic Planning Workshop Documents (continued)*

Action Plan Matrix

Tri-City Parents of the Handicapped Support Network Checklist

- Project description
- Actions timeline
- People responsible
- What? Why?
- How?
- When?
- Who?

Figure 7.   *Strategic Planning Workshop Documents* (*continued*)

and disagree about the board's roles and responsibilities? Is the action-plan matrix sufficient?

Interview someone who has facilitated a strategic planning session. Ask her or him these same questions. Then spend some time creating your own version of the same documents that Leslie did. This would be a good activity for your group or class to practice at a strategic planning workshop or retreat. Finally, does your board of education see its role and responsibilities the same as outlined above?

29. MINI-CASE   2-28

Leslie walked back into her office after lunch with Elizabeth Quiggley and Vernon Franklin, when she noticed the temporary secretary, Nicole Wang, on the telephone and looking rather agitated. Nicole held up her index finger signaling Leslie to wait for one moment.

"Ms. O'Connor. We have a collect call from State Prison. What should I do?"

Leslie thought quickly. "Tell them we don't accept collect calls." Leslie felt pretty good about her quick thinking and walked back to her office.

One minute later Nicole walked into Leslie's office. "We have another collect call from the prison."

"Tell them the same thing," Leslie responded.

Four more collect calls were made to Lancaster Middle School that morning. Leslie turned them all down. The next day Leslie was the first one to arrive at work and found an angry and rough-looking man waiting at the front door.

"Are you the principal here?" the man asked.

Leslie's first thought was to say, "No, I'm the custodian." But she knew she couldn't, so her reply was a quiet, "Yes."

"I've got a bone to pick with you. I'm the guy who kept making collect calls from State Prison, yesterday. Why did you do that?"

In a somewhat stuttering fashion, Leslie said, "Our district has a policy against accepting collect calls."

The man went on, "I was trying to call my son. I have no home phone. I wanted to have my son tell my wife to pick me up, because I was getting out. I had to hitchhike home."

All Leslie could think of to say was, "I'm sorry that happened."

The apology seemed to make a difference. "That's okay, I guess. You know, I was in prison for drug abuse. Now I'm clean. You know, I used to do a clown routine for parties. I want to put my energy into something positive. I will do a healthy-lifestyles assembly for your school for free."

Your Task

Would you have accepted the collect calls? What protocol for such calls does your district have? How would you have handled the man in person?

30. MINI-CASE

Leslie was sure the day couldn't get any worse. She was wrong, because one hour later Nicole asked her to listen to two messages on the school answering machine.

The first message had the voice of a middle-school-age boy. "We put a bomb in the school. It's going to blow up at 9:00." That was it.

The second phone message had the voice of a different middle-school-age boy. In a rather upset tone, the boy said, "We're not kidding, you know!"

As Nicole and Leslie played the tape over and over, Police Liaison Officer Hamilton Freese walked into the office.

"Hamilton, listen to these messages. I know the voices, but I can't place them," Leslie said, anguished.

Your Task

What would you do in this situation? What is district standard operating procedure for bomb threats? Describe each step in these procedures.

31. MINI-CASE

This was not a good day for the Lancaster Middle School principal. She walked back to her office and turned on the radio. The local station had a "free-beer Friday" promotion. The talk-show hosts had asked the listeners to call in if they knew where Otis Redding sang his last concert. Leslie was stunned when she heard who called in.

> The host asked, "And who am I talking to today?"
> "Bob and Terry!" came the enthusiastic response from a youthful voice.
> "Well, Bob and Terry, where are you calling from?"
> "Lancaster Middle School; we're working the school store!"

Your Task

What do you do if you're Leslie, if anything? What policies or rules will you use?

32. CASE STUDY

The afternoon had to be better than the morning, didn't it? Assistant Principal Ron Cartwright knocked on Leslie's door.

> He began, "Leslie, I really blew it."
> "Now Ron, I'm sure it can't be all that bad. What happened?"
> Ron continued, "This is a complex story, so bear with me. You know Tommy Gea; he's been a real pain for much of the year. Well, he is on our school wrestling team and was undefeated. His good work on the team helped to improve his behavior in the classroom. While he's not been an angel, he's been pretty quiet."
> Leslie wanted Ron to get on with it. "Go on."

"Well, after the last match of the regular season, it was reported to one of his teachers—Melissa Korn—that he was at a party drinking. Melissa reported it to me. She told me that two different kids reported it to her. I talked to Tommy. He admitted to being at the party but not drinking."

"I don't like where I think this might be going, Ron," Leslie said.

"I know. I have been so impressed with Tommy's progress that after a great deal of discussion, I talked Melissa into dropping it. I thought that cutting Tommy from the tournament would be devastating to him. Now that the tournament is over, his behavior has plummeted, and other kids are starting to talk about it!"

Leslie had not lost her cool yet this year, but she was about to. "First, Ron, I want you to go back to the policy and follow it. Tommy will have to miss the next three sporting events he's in for the next season. Then, go home. You're suspended for the next three days!"

Ron's mouth dropped open. He looked as if he was trying to say something, but no words were to be found. He turned and walked out of the office.

Your Task

How should Ron have handled the situation from the very beginning? What is your district policy for athletic code violations? Now, critique Leslie's handling of Ron. Was she within her responsibilities to suspend Ron? Talk to your director of personnel or human relations for his or her advice. Is it proper to suspend Tommy from future events after the policy was not followed in the first place?

33. MINI-CASE

The BASD teachers have been working without a ratified contract for a year and a half. Teacher morale is getting seriously low. Guidance counselor Dave Phlander has become good friends with Leslie as they have worked closely together this past year. Leslie relied on the advice of Dave on many occasions. On this morning, Dave caught Leslie in the hallway outside his office.

"Good morning, Leslie. I want to give you a heads-up. The executive board of the BEA has asked all teachers to take a work-to-rule stance starting tomorrow. They are protesting their lack of contract progress."

Leslie's first thought was, "How can they do this to me? I've been so good to them." Fortunately, she did not share these sentiments with Dave. All she could muster was a "Thanks for letting me know, Dave." And she hurried on her way.

Your Task

If this happened to you, what would you do? Who would you contact? What kinds of things would you have to make certain were taken care of? What would be your stance in working with the teachers? Would you make any announcements to staff? To parents?

34. MINI-CASE   2–28

Bill Harwell, reporter of the local newspaper, arrived unannounced at the Lancaster offices. Leslie saw him walk in.

"Hi, Mr. Harwell. What can I do for you this afternoon?"

"I'm working on a news item," Bill said. "One of your students—Tommy Kanton—was arrested for shoplifting and assault this past weekend. I understand that he is receiving special education services, and I want to find out more about this. With the open-records law, I can have access to his files. There's also a rumor circulating that one of his teachers has known about past criminal behavior and has helped to cover it up. I want to look at this teacher's personnel files to see if this has ever been documented and whether or not he has ever been disciplined."

These requests floored Leslie. She didn't think either of these open-records law requests were legitimate. They surely didn't seem to be; at least she hoped such requests weren't permitted. The point was, she didn't know the law.

"I'm sorry, Mr. Harwell. I have never had such a request. I don't know if I can do that. I'll have to check with downtown, first."

Bill Harwell looked at Leslie with the slightest of grins; at least it looked like a grin to Leslie. He decided not to push the issue. "All right, Leslie. Give me a call this afternoon."

Leslie went immediately to her office and picked up the phone.

Your Task

Who would you be calling? Exactly what do the open-records laws in your state permit? Think in terms of students and staff. What safeguards are needed to protect the privacy of staff and students alike?

35. MINI-CASE

Leslie stopped by ED/BD teacher Leo Cranston's room to talk to him about a fund-raiser. She was going to tell him about a phone call she received from an angry parent, when her attention was sidetracked by something she saw taped to the chalkboard. It was an article from the newspaper (see box 14).

The article was disturbing enough to Leslie. But, what was even more disturbing was the fact that a handwritten note was inserted into the article. The student's name, Tommy Kanton, was inserted into the headline of the article.

Leslie ripped the article off the board and confronted Leo. "You can't have this posted on the board!" With that, she threw the article in the wastebasket. Then she ended the conversation with, "See me later about a call I got from a parent about your fund-raiser."

Your Task

Did Leslie act sufficiently? What would you have done under these circumstances?

Box 14   Newspaper Article

Local Youth Arrested for Assault and Robbery

A student at Lancaster Middle School was arrested this past weekend for robbing the Drop-In Mini-Mart on Sherman Blvd. The boy punched and kicked the employee behind the counter and threatened her with a knife. He then rifled through the cash register and stole approximately $350. Charges are pending until the D.A. investigates the crime.

---

36. CASE STUDY

When Leslie picked up the ringing phone, she had no idea how pivotal her response would be to her principalship. On the phone was Tony Mousseli. He had district math coordinator Helen Harnek on his speaker phone.

"Leslie, we've got a little predicament here. It's a conundrum. In 1999, the BASD Board of Education passed a policy stating its full support of site-based management. It took nearly two years for the board to agree, as a couple of board members didn't want to give up centralized power—really their own power, I think. In my opinion, the only reason the policy got passed is the two board members who were stopping this retired from the board."

Helen interjected, "Perhaps they were visionaries. They could foresee such a problem as we have now."

Tony came back, "Helen, could you go ahead and tell Leslie about the other board action—the one in which we now have a conflict?"

"This past spring, Leslie, the Board of Education passed the action that the entire Britton Area School District, K–8, adopt and fully implement the new Virginia-based Hands-On Math Program. This new program is a spiraling format that is seamless with our current high school math curriculum and has been supported by the community and business leaders because it has the math they require."

"Okay, I understand," Leslie said.

"That's not the full story, Leslie," interrupted Tony. "The problem is that we have found out that Lancaster's math department has not accepted this. They say they feel the new program is weak on basics and misses out on many of the fundamentals necessary in math. And they seem to be cloaking their stance under the policy of site-based management."

"What do you mean, Tony?" Leslie asked.

"They say that their site, their department, has decided against the new math and wants to use their old math. And, that's what they've been doing all year. How should we handle this, Leslie? I do want to support site-based management, but I think it's being abused here because some teachers don't want to update their lesson plans. And Helen has tons of research to support her point."

Your Task

Prepare to do this case study as a role-play exercise. Involve Helen, Tony, Leslie, and members of the site-based management team. You will have to decide who will lead this, whether there will be separate meetings, and so on. Feel free to be flexible in how you format your response.

37. MINI-CASE

Assistant Principal Ron Cartwright had sent Leslie an e-mail asking her to stop by his office when she got a chance. He needed to talk to her. Leslie's first chance to stop and talk was at 1:15—during her lunch break.

As she walked into Ron's office, he motioned her to sit down.

> "Leslie, I feel like this is a dead-end job for me. It seems like all I do is discipline the students, monitor their attendance, and make my presence known throughout the day and at after-school events. I really don't do anything of professional consequence. I'm asking you for some help. Can you help me by providing me some other responsibilities so that I can gain some valuable experience as a building administrator—more than a quasi-administrator? I want to be more marketable."
>
> "Gosh, Ron. I never knew," Leslie replied. "I wish you would have told me earlier. I've got some time right now. Let's talk about what you can do and what I might give up."

Your Task

Ron has a concern common to many assistant principals. What are some of the things that a principal should have the assistant principal do? This exercise will be valuable to you as you may well be an assistant principal in your first administrative job.

38. MINI-CASE

By the end of the day, Leo Cranston still had not met with Leslie. So, Leslie walked up to Leo's favorite place for respite—the third-floor men's lounge. She opened the door and was immediately accosted by cigarette smoke. (Smoking on school grounds was not permitted.) But, the lounge was empty. However, an image of someone was present. Leslie noticed a cartoon pin-up—probably from an "adult" magazine—tacked to the wall. Leslie ripped it down and threw it into the wastebasket.

Your Task

Put yourself into Leslie's shoes. How would you handle these issues?

39. CASE STUDY

Ron Cartwright motioned Leslie into his office. He was holding the telephone up to his ear, but about three inches away. Someone was shouting on the other end; Leslie could hear the noise as she stood in the doorway.

> "One moment, sir. Here's the principal. I think she would want to hear this from you." He put his hand over the phone and said to Leslie, "It's Mr. Krankow. He's furious about Leo Cranston's LD class fund-raiser."
>
> Leslie took the phone from Ron. "Hello, Mr. Krankow. This is Leslie O'Connor."
>
> "I'll tell you what. I'm not going to pay the $45," he snorted.
>
> "Can you tell me what this is about, Mr. Krankow?"
>
> "You're goll darn right I will! This past weekend, your flippin' teacher took all the kids to the mall. They were selling candy bars for money so they could do some fun stuff in the classroom. He dropped them off at the mall at 9 a.m. and didn't come back to pick them up until 4 p.m. The kids sold them candy bars in an hour and spent all they earned at the arcade and food court. How can you let that happen?"

After ten more minutes of conversation, Leslie determined that Leo Cranston did indeed take the kids to the mall, drop them off at the front door, and pick them up at the end of the day. Nine ED kids spent the whole day at the mall without any adult supervision. When they got back to school the next day, without the money, Leo Cranston told the kids they would have to pay for the money they wasted.

Your Task

How would you end the telephone conversation with Mr. Krankow? What would you say to Leo Cranston? Any disciplinary action necessary? Do you have any policy to support you? Is this something Ron should handle, or is this clearly a case for the principal?

40. MINI-CASE

Assistant basketball coach Fritz Haggerty stopped by to see Leslie as she ate lunch in the lounge.

> "Fruit and yogurt again, huh, Leslie? I've got a favor to ask of you. Could you sign this form so that I can go to the state basketball tournament?"
> Leslie's reply made everyone in the lounge stop to take pause. "Not so fast, Fritz. Subs are at a premium now. There are days when we don't have enough subs to cover for teachers who call in sick."
> "But, Leslie. This is a tradition; the paperwork is only a formality. All basketball coaches in the middle and high schools go," Fritz said.

The non-coaching staff all had the faintest of smirks on their faces. What was Leslie going to do? How far would she push?

Your Task

How far would you push, if at all? Why? What is your district's policy? What are some innovative ways districts are handling the substitute-teacher crisis?

41. MINI-CASE

Madison Sweeney saw Leslie walking down the hallway and sprinted up to her principal.

> "Hi, Ms. O'Connor! Mrs. Allan said I should talk to you. She wants to reward our class for all getting A's and B's on our end-of-the-quarter test. She said she would show the class a video of our choosing. Our class voted on *The Matrix*, which I have at home. Now, she is

saying she's not so sure about that movie, and that I should ask you. Please, please, please, Ms. O'Connor! Most of us have already seen the movie anyway!"

Leslie was really getting frustrated with all the tedious and petty decisions she was being asked to make. "Why can't people just make wise decisions on their own?" she thought to herself. And, with her busy schedule this year, she had not even heard of this movie. All she could think of saying to Madison was, "I'll have to get back to you."

Your Task

Role-play your follow-up to this scene. Talk to Madison about your decision. Does your school have a policy that will help guide your decision?

42. CASE STUDY

Today, Ron Cartwright was at a meeting for all assistant principals in the BASD. So Leslie would have to handle all the discipline problems. As it turned out, the next incident confounded and embarrassed her.

Nicole stepped into Leslie's office. "Ms. O'Connor! Chris Wheeler is standing in the outer office and refuses to sit, and he's quite angry."

Leslie walked out to see six-foot, two-inch Chris Wheeler standing with his arms crossed against his chest and facing the outer door. "Please come into my office, Chris," Leslie coaxed in a reassuring voice. She hoped he would follow because she didn't know what she would do if he wouldn't follow. But he did.

"What's wrong, today, Chris?" Leslie asked.

"I'm not going to do it anymore!" he huffed.

"What?"

"I'm not going to do it anymore!" Chris repeated with exasperation.

"You're not going to do what anymore, Chris?" Leslie asked calmly.

"I'm not going to stand in the corner in Hamilton's room anymore!"

Leslie was shocked that Frank Hamilton required an eighth-grader to stand in the corner. "How long have you been standing in the corner?" she asked.

"Three weeks!"

Leslie was floored. "Well, that's not going to happen anymore! Let's go." With that, she and Chris marched up three flights of stairs to Hamilton's room.

Leslie opened the door of the darkened classroom. They were watching a *Three Stooges* movie. She and Chris walked back to Frank Hamilton's desk and said, "Chris will no longer be standing in the corner. Handle your discipline problems some other way."

"What should I do? He's totally uncooperative. He is a distraction to all the other students. Seriously now, tell me, what should I do? Should I send him to your office every day?"

Leslie was flummoxed. "You mean he distracts the students from these movies you're always showing? See me after school, and we can talk about some ideas."

Your Task

There are perhaps two or three issues for Leslie to deal with. Identify them and provide responses to them.

43. MINI-CASE

While they are not basketball coaches, several of the men and women teachers are basketball fans. They won't be going to the state high school basketball tournament this week, but they still want to watch the game. Antonio Black enters Leslie's office before the school bell rings.

"Top o' the morning to you, Les. A group of us needs your help. Marion, the librarian, is wound a little too tight. She has denied us the opportunity to watch the Boys State Basketball tournament on the school television sets. Ben Richards always overrode her in the past. All we want is for her to tune in the tournament on the school cable and run it to our classrooms. She says 'District policy says. . .' Will you talk to her?"

"Antonio, I understand where you're coming from," Leslie said. "I think Marion may be right, and she feels put in an awkward position. I'll talk to her."

Your Task

There are several issues here, some subtle and others not so subtle. What are they? How would you handle them?

44. MINI-CASE

School library/media specialist Marion Kope had left a message for Leslie to stop by the media center when she had a chance. Leslie finally was able to get there at 11:15 a.m.

"Good morning, Marion. What can I do for you?"

Marion was red in the face. "Leslie, the teachers' Committee for Positive Discipline wants to reward all the students who have not received a discipline infraction this past quarter by letting them watch a Disney movie. They want me to take a personal copy of *Finding Nemo* and play it through our school cable. This is a copyright infringement, and we're not allowed to do that. The district policy says, and I quote, 'The use of videos other than from the media collection is guided by district and building policy. To avoid copyright law violation, rental video tapes may not be viewed by a class, since this is considered to be public performance.' But I'm getting a lot of pressure from the teachers. They're saying that I'm being too literal and too anal. I'm not going to be a party to this."

Leslie kind of concurred with the teachers, but she didn't want to go against policy or break the law. "I'll have to get back to you on this, Marion."

Your Task

What is your district policy on schoolwide viewing of copyrighted materials? Is this breaking copyright laws? Does this policy, as stated by Marion, clearly and cleanly speak to this case? If not, what is the problem and the solution? Would you take the lead on handling this situation, or would you have Marion take the lead and you play a supportive role? Or is this much ado about nothing?

45. MINI-CASE

Leslie found herself in the middle of what she thought was a longer-than-necessary drop-in visit by a parent of one of her sixth-grade students. Mr. Grant was concerned that the sixth-grade mathematics curriculum allowed for too much use of calculators. The gist of his complaint was that the students were allowed to use calculators to solve problems before they had mastered the fundamental skills and knowledge of basic math.

Leslie really didn't know what to say. She had heard this complaint before but didn't think it was valid. So, she decided to simply listen to Mr. Grant's complaint. She did ask him whether he had talked to the sixth-grade math teacher. He had not. Leslie mentioned that calculator use was part of the curriculum and that she appreciated hearing his concerns. Leslie promised Mr. Grant that she would share his concerns with the staff and the math curriculum coordinator. He seemed fine with this. Leslie figured he just needed to vent a little.

Ironically, half an hour later, Leslie received a phone call from another sixth-grade parent. This parent, Mr. Lamar, had the opposite complaint. He thought that with modern technology, why should we waste time doing tedious rote practice when we could use the technology and more efficiently and effectively teach higher-level mathematics?

This was more in tune with Leslie's philosophy and thinking. She did tell Mr. Lamar of Mr. Grant's concern—but she did not mention his name. She explained to Mr. Lamar that having parents with such different philosophies made it difficult for educators to meet everyone's desires. He understood but stood firm on his beliefs.

After the phone call was over, Leslie decided to set up an appointment with her math teachers and with the district math coordinator—Helen Harnek. She wanted to plan a mini-inservice for parents to talk about the math curriculum.

Your Task

What would you say to these parents? Would you have any follow-up? Do you like the idea of a mini-inservice for parents? If so, how would you structure it?

46. MINI-CASE

Leslie sat down at her kitchen table on this Saturday morning. Her goal was to prepare for her first meeting with the newly formed Lancaster Site Council. Leslie had a goal to get this group up and running earlier, but so many other issues kept putting this task on the back burner. This group was made up of one teacher representative from each department, one teacher representing special education teachers, one teacher representing non-core academic classes, one teacher paraprofessional representing classified staff members, and five parents. This made for a large and cumbersome group, but it appeared to be very representative.

Leslie wanted to have a short agenda, but one that was crucial for the future of this committee. She would start the meeting with introductions. Her next agenda item would be the establishment of ground rules and a decision-making matrix. The agenda would conclude with setting priorities and a charge for the site council for this school year.

With that focus in mind, Leslie began sketching out a framework for her proposed decision-making matrix. She knew that some decisions were definitely her responsibility. On the other hand, she wanted to encourage ownership by members of her site council. This made sense, not only because it provided ownership, but because the staff have more expertise in particular areas—it would be wise for them to make such decisions. Likewise, she wanted to encourage site council members to develop their leadership capacity. Some decisions they could make on their own without her. While sipping on a cup of coffee and nibbling on some homemade peanut butter cookies, Leslie developed the matrix shown in figure 8.

Your Task

How big should a site council be? What do you think would be a good number to have adequate representation without becoming too cumbersome? Would you put students on the site council? What would be their role?

With regard to the decision-making matrix, how do you rate it? Is it too broad and general or too restrictive? Create your own matrix. Sit

Category	Principal Unilateral	Principal with Input	Shared with Site Council	Site Council Unilateral
Personnel	X			
Curriculum	N/A			
Budget		X		
Policies				
Discipline			X	
Staff dev.		X		
Assemblies		X		
Scheduling	X			
Hiring	X			
Other				
Other				
Other				

Figure 8.   *Decision-Making Matrix*

down with your building administrator and see whether he or she uses such a matrix. Does your superintendent and board of education use a matrix for district-level decision-making?

47. MINI-CASE

Math teacher Khamir al-Benzin knocked on Leslie's door. His face looked ashen.

"Leslie," he said.

"What is it, Khamir?" Leslie asked, concerned.

"Every week, for my grad class, I take one of the school's laptop computers for note taking. Leslie, I lost it. On my way home, it struck me that I left it at class. I went back but it was gone. I called the university this morning, first thing, but they couldn't find it. What are we going to do?"

"Oh, Khamir. I don't know. I'll have to check into this and get back to you. Do you have a copy of the request form for personal use of technology?" Leslie didn't know what else to say.

"I never filled out that form."

Your Task

What should Leslie do? Should Khamir receive any punishment? If so, what? Does your school have such a request form? Investigate such a form and how Khamir should be handled.

48. MINI-CASE

As Khamir left Leslie's office, she heard her computer announce, "You've got mail." She turned to look at her e-mail message. It was a note from the human resources director, Frances Williams (see box 15).

Leslie read the e-mail twice. She didn't think this was fair. "All employees should get paid for the work they do at the level they are working," she thought. "Even if this is temporary, this seems unfair."

Besides, Leslie wanted to support her staff. This was an opportunity to stand up for their rights. So, she sent an e-mail reply to Frances. She told her that she would like Frances to reconsider her position and her rationale for it.

Your Task

Who do you think is right, Frances or Leslie? Why? How would such a situation be handled in your district? Either write your e-mail response to Frances explaining why you disagree with her, or write notes to yourself about what you will say to Nicole.

Box 15   Grievance Memo

Leslie,

We've got a grievance from your teacher aide, Nicole Wang. She has been filling in for Georgine Simons. Nicole has said to me that she should be getting paid at the secretary rate since she is doing secretarial work, rather than getting paid at the teacher aide rate. I told her that this is a temporary assignment and that her job status will not change. Therefore, she will continue to get paid at her current rate.

Thanks,
Frances Williams
Director of Human Resources
Britton Area School District

Box 16   Policy Committee Meeting

To: District Technology Policy Committee
From: Michelle Clark, BASD Technology Coordinator
Re: Next Meeting

We will be holding our next committee meeting on Friday after-noon from 1 to 5 p.m. in the Board of Education Room. We need to review the following policies:

1. Web site guidelines
2. Publishing of students' work on the Internet
3. Internet filters
4. Internet use by employees and students (and permissions)

Please review these policies before the meeting. We will be look-ing at whether our current policies need any adjustments, large and small. Be ready to bring your suggestions.

---

49. MINI-CASE

While Leslie was reading her e-mail, she found a note from the district technology coordinator, Michelle Clark (see box 16).

Your Task

Pretend you're Leslie. Review your district policies in these areas and be ready to make suggestions. (This would be an excellent oppor-tunity for a role-play. Your class could choose one district's set of poli-cies and use them for the exercise. You could then run the committee meeting.)

50. CASE STUDY

Leo Cranston was going to be the end of Leslie, or at least that's what she believed. Temporary secretary Nicole Wang walked into the princi-pal's office with some hesitation.

"Ms. O'Connor, I think we may have a problem here. I'm looking at this purchase order from the PTO. Leo Cranston submitted it. Apparently, Mr. Cranston was given $300 from the PTO to go to United Innovative Technologies and purchase a television and DVD player for the school."

"Sure. I was at the PTO meeting when they gave him the money to purchase that equipment. What's the problem?" Leslie asked.

"Well, look at the P.O. He signed it, but it looks as if there is white-out on this one line. I called the manager at United Innovative Technologies and asked him what was on the P.O. Leslie, the manager told me that with that large of a purchase for the school, the store gave us a free microwave oven. I think Leo kept it for himself."

Your Task

How would you investigate this? Who do you need to talk to? What things do you need to consider? (This would be a great role-play.)

51. CASE STUDY

Ron Cartwright brought Amanda Pinkley to Leslie's office.

"Amanda, please wait out here while I talk to Mrs. O'Connor," Ron began. Then he closed the door behind him. He continued, "I've got a new twist on an old story, Les. Amanda was playing with a toy gun on school grounds late yesterday afternoon."

"We've got a policy for that, Ron," Leslie interrupted.

"True, but the circumstances might warrant reconsideration. You see, the toy gun is a cap gun. You know, the kind that makes a loud popping sound, though it kind of looks like a real gun. Well, anyway, she came to watch the end of the intramural softball game. But the game had just finished when she got there. So, she wasn't a part of the school function, and school hours were over. But it was still on school property. Her friends knew she was just playing, but other people could have been scared. With those circumstances, do we still follow the policy?"

"Let's take a look at the policy, Ron." Leslie pulled out her copy of the district weapons policy (see box 17).

Box 17   Britton Area School District Weapons Policy

The Britton Area School District expressly forbids the possession or use of any and all weapons and look-alike weapons on school grounds or at school functions. State law dictates that all such violations are to be considered misdemeanors (in the case of look-alikes) and felonies (in the case of actual weapons). All instances must be reported to the local law enforcement agencies.

The list of weapons and look-alike weapons includes, but may not be limited to: guns, pellet guns, knives, pocket knives, razor blades, arrows (except school property), martial arts devices, and any other item that is intended to intimidate or harm another person.

Upon referral to school administration, the following people must be contacted: police liaison officer (according to regulations of the Gun-Free Schools Act), district administrator, and the student's parents.

The school principal will be responsible for implementing disciplinary measures. In all nonthreatening instances, the student will receive an automatic three-day out-of-school suspension. All threatening instances will require the immediate processing procedures for expulsion.

Adopted: 3/21/99
Revised: 8/29/03

"Ron, the answer seems clear to me," Leslie said. "Amanda was on school grounds. The policy makes that clear, and she must be suspended for three days. Furthermore, you must report this to the police."

Your Task

Do you agree with Leslie's interpretation? Could this policy be interpreted another way? What are the strengths and weaknesses of this policy? Examine your school district's policy for weapons. In light of the preceding scenario, what action would your policy dictate?

52. MINI-CASE

Leslie was paged on her two-way radio to the bank of lockers on the north wing of the second floor. When she arrived, she saw C. J. Allen standing in the hall with a student, Ed Payne.

> C. J. walked right up to Leslie. "Le . . . Ms. O'Connor, we're having a bit of a problem here. Two of my outstanding students told me that Ed has marijuana in his locker. Ed denies this but refuses to open up his locker."
>
> In a very agitated tone, Ed interjected, "I want to know who is telling these lies on me! I know my rights!"

Leslie was truly caught off guard. She did not know the school's search-and-seizure policy.

Your Task

What would you do if you were in Leslie's shoes? What does your district policy say about search and seizure of student lockers? Their persons? Their vehicles? What does your policy say about use of police dogs, metal detectors, and breath screening? What are your district guidelines about student interviews and interrogations and parent notification? Can you divulge the names of the students who told on Ed?

Case Categories

Budget
Communication
Curriculum
Emergency
Ethics
Parent/Community Relations
Personnel
Philosophical Position
Policy Analysis
Professional Development
Routine Operations
Staff-Parent Relations
Staff Relations
Student Issues

List of Cases

Case No.	Type	Category	Description
1.	Mini-Case	Communication	memo to staff
2.	Mini-Case	Communication	letter to parents
3.	Mini-Case	Routine Operations	to-do list
4.	In-Baskets		
1.		Routine Operations	anonymous phone call
2.		Curriculum/Parent Relations	letter from parent
3.		Communication	call from board pres.
4.		Communication/ Philosophical Position	letter from concerned citizens group
5.		Community Relations	call from newspaper
6.		Community Relations/ Budget	State Taxpayers' Alliance
7.		Budget/Routine Operations	budget reduction request
8.		Routine Operations	playground repairs
9.		Community Relations	concerned neighbor
10.		Routine Operations	student arrivals
11.		Personnel	concerned teacher
12.		Community Relations	invitation to speak
13.		Routine Operations	advertising
5.	Mini-Case	Personnel	intensive assistance
6.	Mini-Case	Professional Development	meeting with mentor
7.	Case Study	Professional Development	contract language
8.	Case Study	Philosophical Position/ Staff-Parent Relations	parent requests
9.	Mini-Case*	Parent Relations	assembly request
10.	Case Study	Routine Operations	bad boiler
11.	Case Study*	Community Relations	newspaper interview
12.	Case Study	Student Issues/ Policy Analysis	student neglect
13.	Mini-Case	Student Issues/ Policy Analysis	discipline forms
14.	Mini-Case	Personnel/ Professional Development	impromptu observation

Case No.	Type	Category	Description
15.	Case Study*	Personnel/ Community Relations	teacher error
16.	Case Study*	Emergency	marital dispute hits
17.	In-Baskets		
	1.	Personnel	grievance
	2.	Routine Operations	technology misuse
	3.	Staff Relations	administrative event
	4.	Ethics	free tickets
	5.	Routine Operations	challenged book
	6.	Personnel	secretary quits
	7.	Routine Operations/ Community Relations	angry parent
	8.	Personnel/ Community Relations	absent teacher
	9.	Community Relations	lawsuit from parent
	10.	Routine Operations	graffiti
	11.	Student Issues/ Philosophical Position	middle finger
	12.	Personnel/ Student Issues	staff behavior
	13.	Personnel/ Student Issues	discipline
18.	Mini-Case	Professional Development	administrative evaluation
19.	Case Study	Policy Analysis	sexual harassment
20.	Case Study*	Curriculum/ Parent Relations	human growth and development curriculum
21.	Case Study	Policy Analysis	board meeting
22.	Case Study*	Policy Analysis	challenged materials
23.	Case Study	Policy Analysis	truancy
24.	Case Study*	Curriculum/ Community Relations	Christmas program
25.	Case Study	Routine Operations	budget preparations
26.	In-Baskets		
	1.	Personnel	drunken lunch lady
	2.	Student Issues/ Philosophical Position	LD grades
	3.	Student Issues/ Community Relations	store problems
	4.	Student Issues/ Personnel	lunch complaint
	5.	Personnel	travel request
	6.	Communication	note from superintendent
	7.	Personnel	travel request
	8.	Communication	speaking request
	9.	Student Issues	spider in class
	10.	Curriculum/ Parent Relations	family trip
	11.	Routine Operations	lost snake
	12.	Student Issues	prayer group
	13.	Student Issues	questionable T-shirt

Case No.	Type	Category	Description
27.	Mini-Case	Personnel/ Policy Analysis	job posting
28.	Case Study	Routine Operations	strategic planning
29.	Mini-Case*	Routine Operations	collect calls
30.	Mini-Case	Policy Analysis/ Emergency	bomb threat
31.	Mini-Case*	Policy Analysis	free-beer Friday
32.	Case Study*	Policy Analysis/ Student Issues	athletic code
33.	Mini-Case	Personnel	work-to-rule
34.	Mini-Case*	Student Issues/ Policy Analysis	open-records request
35.	Mini-Case*	Personnel/ Student Issues	misconduct
36.	Case Study*	Policy Analysis	conflicting policies
37.	Mini-Case	Personnel	job duties
38.	Mini-Case	Personnel	lounge behavior
39.	Case Study*	Personnel	fund-raiser problem
40.	Mini-Case	Policy Analysis	substitute crisis
41.	Mini-Case*	Policy Analysis	video
42.	Case Study*	Personnel	discipline
43.	Mini-Case	Policy Analysis/ Personnel	entertainment
44.	Mini-Case	Policy Analysis	copyright
45.	Mini-Case*	Curriculum	calculators
46.	Mini-Case	Policy Analysis	site council
47.	Mini-Case	Personnel	lost computer
48.	Mini-Case	Personnel	grievance
49.	Mini-Case	Policy Analysis	technology policies
50.	Case Study	Personnel	misappropriations
51.	Case Study	Policy Analysis/ Student Issues	weapons
52.	Mini-Case*	Policy Analysis/ Student Issues	search and seizure

* These items lend themselves to role-plays.

References

Freire, P. 2002. *Pedagogy of the oppressed.* New York: Continuum.

Glickman, C., S. Gordon, and J. M. Ross-Gordon. 1998. *Supervision of instruction: A developmental approach.* Boston: Allyn & Bacon.

Goleman, D. March 2000. Leadership that gets results. *Harvard Business Review,* 78–90.

Hayles, N. K. 1991. *Chaos and order: Complex dynamics in literature and science.* Chicago: University of Chicago Press.

Hersey, P., and K. Blanchard. 1988. *Management of organizational behavior: Utilizing human resources.* 6th ed. Upper Saddle River, N.J.: Prentice Hall.

House, R., and T. Mitchell. 1974. A path-goal theory of leader effectiveness. *Journal of Contemporary Business,* 3, 81–97.

Kotter, J. P. 1999. *What leaders really do.* Cambridge, Mass.: Harvard Business School Press.

Owens, R. G. 2004. *Organizational behavior in education: Adaptive leadership and school reform.* Boston: Pearson-Allyn & Bacon.

Rettig, P. R. 2002. *Quantum leaps in school leadership.* Lanham, Md.: Scarecrow Education.

Sergiovanni, T., and R. J. Starratt. 2002. *Supervision: A redefinition.* Boston: McGraw-Hill.

Index

Blanchard, Kenneth, xiii

case studies and in-baskets: need for, vii; preparation for; x–xv
case study and in-basket: activities. *See* list of Cases; approach, vii–ix; categories, 79
collaborative, xii
conflict management approaches, xiv

decision-making approaches, xiv–xv
differentiated supervision model, xi–xii

Freire, Paulo, viii

Glickman, Carl, xi, xii
Goleman, Dan, xiii
Gordon, Stephen, xi, xii

Hayles, N. Katherine, and *Chaos and Order: Complex Dynamics in Literature and Science*, viii
Hersey, Paul, xiii
House, Robert, xiii

Kotter, John, xi

leadership styles or approaches, xii–xiv
list of cases, 81–83

managers and leaders, difference between, xi
McGregor, Douglas, x
Mitchell, Terrence, xiii

Owens, Robert, vii

Path–Goal Contingency Model, xiii
Proust, Marcel, xv

Ross-Gordon, Jovita, xi, xii

Sergiovanni, Thomas, xii
Situational Leadership Model, xiii
Starratt, Robert, xii
Stoicheff, Peter, and "The Chaos of Metafiction," viii
supervisor's platform, xii

Theory X, x
Theory Y, x

About the Author

Perry R. Rettig earned his Ph.D. in administrative leadership and supervision from Marquette University in Milwaukee, Wisconsin. He is currently a certified district administrator, principal, and elementary school teacher in that state. For the past seven years he has been an associate professor of educational administration and leadership, as well as the coordinator of the Educational Leadership Program at the University of Wisconsin–Oshkosh. Rettig is also the author of *Quantum Leaps in School Leadership* (ScarecrowEducation 2002).